MURIEL SAVILLE-TROIKE

Georgetown University

Foundations for Teaching English as a Second Language

Second Language

theory and method
for multicultural education

PRENTICE-HALL, INC., *Englewood Cliffs, New Jersey*

Library of Congress Cataloging in Publication Data

SAVILLE-TROIKE, MURIEL, 1936–
    Foundations for teaching English as a second
language.

    Includes bibliographies.
    1. English language—Study and teaching—
Foreign students. I. Title.
PE1128.S28   428'.007   75–33148
ISBN   0-13-329946-5

© 1976 by PRENTICE-HALL, INC.,
Englewood Cliffs, New Jersey

Printed in the United States of America

10   9   8

PRENTICE-HALL INTERNATIONAL, INC., *London*
PRENTICE-HALL OF AUSTRALIA, PTY. LTD., *Sydney*
PRENTICE-HALL OF CANADA, LTD., *Toronto*
PRENTICE-HALL OF INDIA PRIVATE LIMITED, *New Delhi*
PRENTICE-HALL OF JAPAN, INC., *Tokyo*
PRENTICE-HALL OF SOUTHEAST ASIA (PTE.) LTD., *Singapore*

Contents

7
STRATEGIES FOR INSTRUCTION   98

8
THE ROLE OF ESL IN BILINGUAL EDUCATION   129

9
PREPARATION FOR TEACHING   136

APPENDIX   144

Preface

During the past decade, rapid changes have taken place in linguistics, in education, and in the very nature of American society, which have had profound implications for the teaching of English as a second language. Much of the traditional content of ESL programs and materials has been rendered obsolete by these changes, and the goals and methods of ESL instruction have been called seriously into question. The assumptions regarding the nature of language and language learning upon which ESL methodology was founded have been in large part discredited, and special ESL classes in the public schools have been determined to be educationally unsound in many instances, and in possible violation of desegregation laws and decrees. ESL, formerly the handmaiden of assimilation, has found itself in the unfamiliar role of partner with vernacular instruction in the context of education for a pluralistic society.

There is an urgent need to formulate a new set of goals, methods, and concepts for ESL instruction if it is to remain viable and make its potential contribution to American education. The present work draws on recent developments in linguistics, psychology, anthropology, and language pedagogy in an attempt to provide a theoretical basis for such a new formulation. At the same time it draws on my own classroom experiences in teaching non-English speaking students, from the children of migrant laborers in kindergarten to foreign students in college, to suggest practical procedures and strategies for implementing the new directions which are called for.

Most of the background information and instructional strategies presented here are meant to apply primarily to heterogeneous, integrated classes rather than to segregated ESL classes or to English as a foreign language (EFL) programs in other countries, though much of what is said is obviously relevant to them as well. I have also placed emphasis on the role of ESL in bilingual education, explaining their compatible and over-lapping goals and procedures as well as their unique methods and con-tributions. There have been unfortunate misunderstandings in both of these areas regarding their relationship, and too little practical classroom assistance has been available for English teaching which is appropriate to these contexts.

Because a child's first years in school are critical in terms of his self-image, his attitudes toward learning and his wider environment, I have placed a heavy emphasis on early language development and on the acquisition of academic skills (such as reading) at the kindergarten and early elementary levels. At the same time, however, I have attempted to provide suggestions for solving specific problem situations which are likely to occur at a number of different levels. While there are some com-monalties in teaching English as a second language across all age groups, there are also many differences which need to be taken into account. Any apparent redundancies in the text are purposeful rather than inadvert-ent, and are intended to reinforce points regarded as important.

This book has been written both for teachers and for teachers-in-training, especially those interested in ESL and bilingual education, but also for teachers in self-contained classrooms, and for teachers of reading, mathematics, social studies, and other subject areas who have one or more students learning English as a second language while also needing to learn the content of instruction. My aim has been to make current perti-nent information from a number of fields accessible to readers who have little or no previous background in these fields. Because the treatment of each subject is necessarily very abbreviated, I would hope that readers would pursue further information through the additional sources which have been suggested after each topic.

The teacher of English to speakers of other languages has a special trust, and a special responsibility. The student who comes to us exposes more than just his lack of command of a subject. So deeply is language bound up with a person's sense of self-identity and self-worth, that the chances for psychological and social damage to students in the teaching process are very great. In addition, language is not merely an object or a skill, but is the very medium through which much subsequent learning will take place, including the learning of language itself. A great deal of a student's academic, social, and economic opportunity depends upon his control of English, but if it is gained at the cost of the individual's most deeply held values, the gain may not be worth the loss. It is my sincere hope that this book may contribute to helping teachers to teach more effectively, and more sensitively, and to realize more fully the depth of their responsibility in teaching that most human of human traits—language.

No book such as this is created in a vacuum, and I am deeply indebted to many teachers and colleagues for suggestions and insights which have influenced the evolution of my own theory and practice in teaching English as a second language. While I could not possibly name them all, I would like particularly to mention and thank Frederick Brengelman, Archibald A. Hill, Mary Finocchiaro, Robert Lado, John C. Manning, Christina Bratt Paulston, Wilga Rivers, and Rudolph C. Troike. I would also like to express my appreciation to the very competent editorial and production staff of Prentice-Hall who have been of great help: Marilyn Brauer, Fred Bernardi, and Cynthia Insolio.

M. S-T.

From Melting Pot to Salad Bowl

CHAPTER 1

Give me your tired, your poor,
Your huddled masses yearning to breathe free . . .
—from the sonnet "THE NEW COLOSSUS,"
by EMMA LAZARUS

This verse, found on the base of the Statue of Liberty in New York harbor, expresses the philosophy which has dominated the concept of America for the past two centuries. To a Europe torn by war and weighed down by political oppression and rigid class barriers, America was indeed a land of opportunity, where a man's status was determined by his ability rather than his birth, and where the Constitution protected his personal liberty.

The American dream was a reality for many; millions came to our shores seeking to become a part of this new nation and gladly put behind them the languages and cultures they had left, to embrace the new. The passing of the frontier ended the seemingly infinite capacity of the continent to absorb new immigrants, and quotas were imposed, which though biased were still generous. Even today probably no nation on earth admits as many immigrants, nor has so many who wish to come.

Much has been made in recent years of the "myth" of the melting pot. But for many groups for many years it was—and for many still remains—a cherished goal. Millions of people have willingly melted into the mainstream, often contributing something of themselves as they did so.

1

Our national motto, *e pluribus unum*, "out of many, one" can serve to describe our cultural and linguistic sources as well as our political origins. Although our institutions and values reflect the heavy influence of our heritage from England, our national culture is not the invention of a single ethnic group; rather it is a rich amalgam to which many groups have contributed. Terms such as *skunk* and *moccasin, mesa* and *rodeo, chow* and *bayou* bear the stamp of the American experience, and distinguish American English from British English (just as, for example, the varieties of Spanish spoken in Puerto Rico, Cuba, and Mexico differ from that of Spain and reflect the unique history of each of these places).

In most cases, the many immigrant groups to the United States (the Irish, German, Greek, Polish, Czech, Russian, Scandinavian, Italian, and others) wanted to assimilate to the dominant culture, and generally succeeded economically, linguistically, and politically by the second generation of residence. Children often could not talk to their grandparents, so rapidly and completely was the transition to English completed.

Other non-English-speaking communities did not move to the United States; rather, it moved to them: the Native Americans, the original Spanish-speaking in the former Mexican territory of the Southwest, the Acadian French transplanted from Canada to Louisiana, and most recently the Puerto Ricans via our island conquest. Whether they have rejected or been refused assimilation by the dominant society, these diverse speech communities have maintained their linguistic and cultural identity for generations. The "melting-pot" concept has not fully applied to them.

As the United States reaches its bicentennial, we are conscious that we have as a nation begun to mature, and with maturity has come greater sophistication and self-awareness. We have begun to realize that the American dream, which was and is real, has not been equally available to all, and we have begun, however haltingly, to do something about the inequities. Some of us have also begun to recognize that being American does not necessarily mean rejecting our natal languages and cultures, but that successful and satisfying bilingualism and biculturalism are possible in our society. These new realizations reflect one of the most profound changes ever to take place in our national values, and it is important that we understand some of the implications of this change, including both its promises and its problems.

As we look to the experience of history, we find that a certain amount of cultural and linguistic uniformity is a necessary prerequisite for achieving stability in the process of building a nation-state. Linguistic and cultural differences are a great obstacle to national unity, and to full participation by all groups in the national life. At a recent meeting sponsored by the Canadian Commission for UNESCO, African delegates repeatedly made this point: bilingual education is a luxury which only a developed and secure society such as the United States can afford. Even in purely economic terms, most countries cannot afford the cost of developing educational programs in several languages, particularly when they can barely afford to provide an educational system in one. Politically, we must be concerned with the potential centrifugal effects of separatism on our social fabric.

We have few guides as to the ability of truly multilingual and multicultural societies to survive. In the past, most such nations have been conquest states and have lasted only so long as a central government was powerful enough to maintain control—usually by force of arms. We have only to read the newspapers to know how many minority languages are suppressed in nations around the globe—Welsh in England, Breton in France, Basque in France and Spain are examples—and how often linguistic differences lead to bloody clashes, as in Belgium and India. Although with respect to some of our minorities mentioned above, the United States too is a conquest state, the American experience is largely unique both because we are a democracy, and because so many of our non-English-speaking groups came here by choice. Our past history and our present situation are therefore largely without precedent, and a resolution of the problems inherent in a policy of cultural self-determination will require much sincere attention and dedication.

While we cannot deny the *historical* validity of the melting-pot concept—in spite of the fact that not all groups fully melted—nor indeed the *necessity* of developing common cultural institutions in the process of building a nation, we must recognize that we have entered a new period in American history, for which a new metaphor is appropriate—that of the salad bowl.[1] This metaphor is particularly apt, for a salad is not just a mere mechanical mixture of elements; it is rather an emergent entity which is more than the sum of its parts, in which the parts remain distinguishable and we can still recognize their separate contribution to the whole. It is this integrity of our cultural components, then, and their identifiability, which forms the basis of the new metaphor.

The salad-bowl concept of American society is a relatively new one, and like all new ideas, will take time to mature, to be institutionalized, and to spread. It expresses a rich fulfillment of the purposes for which our nation was founded, yet one which will require many readjustments in the equilibrium of our present system of national values and cul-

---

[1] The term "salad bowl" was used by Bambi Cárdenes at a meeting on Mexican-American education held by the United States Commission on Civil Rights in San Antonio, Texas, in March 1974.

tural institutions. As civic violence from Little Rock to Boston has attested, these readjustments by dominant segments of the society do not come easily. Nor have they, much as we might have wished, sprung from an enlightened sense of justice and humanity toward all our citizens. Rather they have resulted from militancy by minority groups demanding equal rights, and from court orders sometimes enforced by federal bayonets—even against a governor standing in a schoolhouse door.

We still have a long way to go before all of the minorities in our country enjoy equal rights, equal access to opportunities, and equal standards of living. As government statistics repeatedly show, there continues to be a vastly disproportionate distribution of minorities with respect to almost any measure of income, health, education, or occupation. Until these inequities have been righted, the American dream will remain for many more of an ideal than a reality.

Inherent in the vision of America expressed by the salad-bowl metaphor is a new approach to education which finds expression in two related movements, bilingual–bicultural education and multicultural education. These movements have their roots in two sources: the demand by minority groups to the right to their cultural integrity, and a humanistic concern for both equal educational opportunity for all children and increased understanding and respect for the cultural diversity in our midst. Taken together, bilingual–bicultural education and multicultural education constitute probably the single most significant movement in the history of American education.

For the child from a non-English-speaking background, language is at the heart of equal access to educational and economic opportunity. English is the national tongue of the United States, and a command of it is essential for full participation in the academic, economic, and political systems of this country. Yet many thousands of children enter our schools each year unable to speak the language. If these students are to have a chance for success in our society, a chance to defend themselves from exploitation, or even a chance to be free to manage their own affairs, they must become fluent in English. To be able to deal with the majority culture on their own terms, they must master most of the basic grammatical structures of English, its sounds, and an adequate English vocabulary, as well as fundamental reading and writing skills, and they must acquire a knowledge of how to use all of these appropriately in a variety of social settings to acquire information and to express themselves.

Different groups and different individuals have a variety of reasons for seeking, or rejecting, the attainment of a fluent command of English as their goal. Apart from the decisions which a group or individual may make, however, the courts have decreed that it is discriminatory for the schools, as public agencies, to require achievement in English of students from non-English-speaking backgrounds without making special provision for them.[2] Thus the schools are under a mandate to provide such students with the linguistic means necessary for their equal access to educational opportunity. Whatever form this provision may take in particular schools, it will inevitably involve some special attention to improving the English skills of these students.

The primary concern of this book is to lay out the foundations which teachers should have to help them more effectively meet this need. These foundations include first of all understanding of the linguistic, cultural, social, and psychological dimensions of the situation, as the basis from which any valid methodology must spring. Although many of the methodological directions reflect the results of practical classroom experience, it is a basic premise of this book that the teacher who understands the factual and conceptual foundations of second language teaching in a cross-cultural setting will be much better prepared to apply the methodology in appropriate ways to meet the needs of the individual student than will a teacher who has been given only a mechanical set of procedures to follow.

If we are to realize the goals of providing equal educational opportunity to children who come from other language backgrounds, we must first learn to accept their existing linguistic and cultural patterns as strengths to build upon, rather than as handicaps to successful learning. We must begin with an understanding of language and culture, because children do not begin learning when they come to school. They are part of a social community, and have already learned much of its values and its expectations. They have acquired communication skills in at least one language, and these are already related to ways of thinking and feeling and acting. Even more importantly perhaps, it should be remembered that the school forms only a part of students' larger learning experience, and that they will continue throughout their school years to learn more outside than in it.

We must recognize such facts as the following:

> Teachers as well as children come with culturally determined individual and group attitudes, expectations, and skills.
>
> Non-English-speaking children usually have different experiences from the ones assumed or desired by the school; the school is thus a cross-cultural learning situation for them.

---

[2]This was the conclusion of the United States Supreme Court in the case of Lau vs. Nichols on January 21, 1974. This decision is of such critical importance for teaching English as a second language, it is included in its entirety as an appendix (see p. 144).

Unconsciously held attitudes and expectations cause teachers to react differently to linguistically and culturally diverse children.

Children's self-image and their achievement levels are strongly influenced by the view and expectations which the majority culture holds of them.

For these reasons, we will first discuss some of the common misconceptions and stereotypes held by the majority culture which may inhibit teachers' real understanding of the non-English-speaking child, and therefore his education. Methods and materials for classroom instruction are, of course, important as well, but they will be addressed later when we may do so critically from a vantage point of psychological, linguistic, and cultural awareness. Finally, special attention will be given to the role of teaching English as a second language in bilingual education programs, and to questions of preparing ourselves or others for the changing requirements of multicultural education.

FOR ADDITIONAL READING

AARONS, ALFRED C., BARBARA Y. GORDON, and WILLIAM A. STEWART, eds., "Linguistic–Cultural Differences and American Education," special anthology issue, *The Florida FL Reporter*, 7, no. 1 (Spring/Summer 1969).

ABRAHAMS, ROGER D. and RUDOLPH C. TROIKE, eds., *Language and Cultural Diversity in American Education* (Englewood Cliffs, N.J.: Prentice-Hall, Inc., 1972).

ALATIS, JAMES E., ed., *Bilingualism and Language Contact: Anthropological, Linguistic, Psychological, and Sociological Aspects*, Monograph Series on Language and Linguistics, No. 23 (Washington, D.C.: Georgetown University Press, 1970).

FISHMAN, JOSHUA A., *Language Loyalty in the United States* (The Hague: Mouton, 1966).

Psychological Foundations

CHAPTER 2

THE NATURE OF LANGUAGE LEARNING

Given appropriate motivation, a normal child can learn any language to which he has adequate exposure. If he hears and responds to two (or more) languages in his environment, he will become bilingual.

Much of a child's language development is completed before he ever comes to school. By the age of six months an infant has produced all of the vowel sounds and most of the consonant sounds of any language in the world, including some that do not occur in the language his parents speak. If the child hears English spoken around him, he will learn to discriminate among those sounds that make a difference in the meaning of English words (the *phonemes*), and he will learn to disregard those that do not. If the child hears Spanish spoken around him, he will learn to discriminate among some sounds the English speaker learns to ignore, as the single *r* in *pero* 'but' and the doubled *r* in *perro* 'dog', and to disregard some differences that are not distinctive in Spanish, but vital to English word-meaning, as the *sh* and *ch* of *share* and *chair*.

The average child has mastered most of the distinctive sounds of his first language before he is three years old, and he controls most of its basic grammatical patterns before he is five or six. Complex grammatical patterns continue to develop through the school years, and he will add new vocabulary items even through adult life.

This feat seems little short of miraculous, and we are not at all sure how it is accomplished. The nature of our speculations has changed radically in the past decade, primarily owing to recent developments in theoretical linguistics and psycholinguistics. These hypotheses have extensive implications for language development programs used during the beginning years of school.

It has been suggested by some that primary language acquisition is in large part the result of the child's natural desire to please his doting parents, who wait impatiently for him to utter a recognizable word. Yet the offspring of even relatively indifferent parents acquire language, as do children of parents who are completely deaf, if there is another at least minimal source of language in their environment. (We are speaking here of hearing children learning the oral expression of language; either hearing or deaf children may acquire language through exposure to the visual mode of expression, sign language.)

It has been suggested by others that a child's language acquisition is purposive, that he develops language because of his urge to communicate his wants and needs to his caretakers. Research indicates, however, that talking develops as an activity that a child indulges in to a great extent for its own sake. Up to the age of about eighteen months, "talk" tends to accompany action or activity rather than be a substitute for it.[1] Within the child's limited sphere of activity, communicative needs seem to be satisfied by gesture and such extralinguistic vocalization as squeals, whines, grunts, and cries.

Perhaps the most widely held view is that a child learns language by imitation (the behaviorist stimulus–response theory). It is true that much of a child's initial language learning can be attributed to his imitation of sounds and words around him, but many of his utterances are quite original and cannot be explained as imitations at all. This stimulus–response theory also holds that the adult's role is to correct the child when he is wrong in his language use and to reinforce him when he is right. In fact, there seems to be no evidence that either correction or reinforcement of phonology and grammar occurs often enough to be an important factor. Parents do correct taboo expressions and misstatements of fact, but seldom correct immature grammatical forms.[2] The same infrequency of correction is found from India to Samoa.[3]

[1] Arnold Gesell, *The First Five Years of Life* (New York: Harper and Row, 1940).

[2] Vivian M. Horner, "The Verbal World of the Lower-Class Three-Year-Old: A Pilot Study in Linguistic Ecology" (unpublished doctoral dissertation, University of Rochester, 1968); Roger Brown, Courtney Cazden, and Ursula Bellugi, "The Child's Grammar from 1 to 3," in *1967 Minnesota Symposium on Child Psychology*, ed. J. P. Hill (Minneapolis, Minn.: University of Minnesota Press, 1969).

[3] Dan I. Slobin, "Questions of Language Development in Cross-Cultural Perspective" (paper prepared for a symposium on Language Learning in Cross-Cultural Perspective, Michigan State University, 1968).

How, then, is language learned?

THE ROLE OF "NATURAL" ABILITY

Language is uniquely human.   Animal noises relate to biological states and processes, such as hunger, courting, danger signals, and anger. Animals cannot be trained to use these noises inappropriately; that is, they cannot switch noises and use one in a situation which would normally call for another.[4]

Further, although the great apes evidently have a limited physiological capacity to produce a few speech sounds and some chimpanzees have learned to communicate by sign language or computer terminal, none has developed anywhere near the skill of even a three-year-old child. And all of us who talk regularly to cats or dogs know that no matter how rich a linguistic environment we provide, we never get even one word in return. (The apparent exception of parrots and certain other birds is only apparent, since they cannot freely combine words or phrases they have learned to produce meaningful new utterances.)

Children have an inherent predisposition to learn language. An innate capacity must be assumed in order to explain several facts:

Children around the world begin to learn their native language at the same age, in much the same way, and in essentially the same sequence.

Children have acquired most of the basic operations in language by the age of four, regardless of their language or social environment.

Children can understand and create novel utterances; they are by no means limited to repeating what they have heard, and many child speech patterns are systematically different from those of the adults around them.

In viewing the ability to acquire language in terms of genetic predisposition, we are saying that part of language structure is genetically "given" to every human child. All languages are incredibly complex systems which no child could possibly *learn* in his early years, in the usual sense of the word, to the degree he exhibits mastery over it. A child's ability to create new sentences is remarkable, and his ability to recognize when a string of common words does *not* constitute a grammatical sentence in the language, is even more so. For example, he can recognize that *Milk me give* is ungrammatical. He has never been told, surely, that

---

[4]Eric H. Lenneberg, "The Capacity for Language Acquisition," in *Readings in Applied Transformational Grammar,* ed. Mark Lester (New York Holt, Rinehart and Winston, 1970).

that particular group of words is not an English sentence, but he knows. If a child had to consciously learn the set of abstract principles that indicate which groups of words are sentences in his language as opposed to those that are not, only the smartest would learn to talk, and it would take them many more years than it does.

A hypothesis for which there is a good deal of support is that a great many of these abstract principles are common to all language, as opposed to the principles that are language-specific, that is, specific to particular languages. According to this view, those principles that are universal are "programmed" into each human child just by virtue of his being human and would account for a child's ability to process the smorgasbord of sounds and words that he hears and come up with essentially the same structures (in the same sequence) as every other child.[5]

There is a definite sequence to language development. We may view the child's development in his first language as a gradual process of acquiring a more and more complex set of rules for generating the sentences of the language. The stages of acquisition tend to correlate closely with maturational development. In the earlier periods of growth, at least, maturation seems to be more reliably definable in terms of motor development than chronological age.

Because the levels of language development can be delineated and studied, it is possible to talk about "child grammar," that is, to describe the kinds of sentences a child can produce or understand at a given maturational level.[6] The differences between these sentences and those used by adults are not viewed as failures on the part of the child, but are considered the normal output of the child's grammar at that level of development. As the child matures, so do his language abilities. Since certain grammatical processes are more complex than others, they require a higher maturational level than simpler ones. In order to master complexities in his first language which are beyond his present linguistic grasp, what the normal child needs is additional time, not additional stimuli.[7]

Linguists probably know more about the child's acquisition of his phonological system than they do about other aspects of first language learning. The first sounds an infant makes are reflexive (at zero to three

---

[5] See especially the writings of Noam Chomsky, Eric Lenneberg, and David McNeil.

[6] Paula Menyuk, *Sentences Children Use* (Cambridge, Mass.: The M.I.T. Press, 1969).

[7] Jean Piaget, *The Language and Thought of the Child* (Cleveland, Ohio: The World Publishing Co., 1955).

months) and associated with physiological states. During the next "babbling" period (from three to twelve months), he demonstrates almost unlimited phonetic capability, producing sounds that will have no later use in his language. When a child first begins to distinguish meaningful speech sounds, it is as though he recognizes only one consonant and one vowel (with any consonant sound or any vowel sound serving in these roles), and can produce words like 'mama', 'gaga', etc. The next step is differentiating between major groups of consonants and vowels such as labial consonants (like *m*) versus nonlabial consonants (like *d*), and front vowels (as in *see*) versus back vowels (as in *saw*).

The process of distinguishing sounds continues until the child has mastered the whole inventory of phonemes in the language. The pairs *t:k, th:f, w:r,* and *l:y* are often problems in English because of their acoustic similarity. The most dissimilar sounds in a child's language are distinguished first, and the most similar last. Most sounds are controlled by age three, and all by the age of about seven, although different children will differ in the exact timing and order of acquisition. (It is important to remember that all figures given represent averages, which implies that there is a normal curve of development, with some children developing sooner, others later.)

Semantics, or meaning, is basic to all language learning. Roger Brown suggests that the first meanings are an extension of Piaget's "sensorimotor intelligence."[8] A child is innately capable of distinguishing objects, recognizing relationships, and learning that environmental experiences can be expressed with language. All children in the first stage of language acquisition (eighteen to twenty-four months), whatever their first language, have the same repertoire of operations and relations to express these operations. These include naming, negation, action and object, location, possession, and attribute.

In the second stage, children learn noun and verb inflections, means for expressing spatial relations, and some helping verbs (auxiliaries), as well as basic word order. Although most basic structures have been acquired by four or five, the acquisition of syntax continues at least through age ten and perhaps never terminates completely.[9]

The rate of progression through these and subsequent stages will vary radically among individual children, but the order of development is generally invariant for both different children and different languages. The rate may be influenced by family interaction and other social,

---

[8]Roger Brown, *A First Language: The Early Stages* (Cambridge, Mass.: Harvard University Press, 1973).

[9]Carol Chomsky, *The Acquisition of Syntax in Children from 5 to 10* (Cambridge, Mass.: The M.I.T. Press, 1969).

psychological, and cultural variables; the order is "primarily determined by the relative semantic and grammatical complexity of constructions."[10]

There is a cutoff point for language development.   Progress in language development usually begins to slow sharply at about the age of puberty—no matter what level has been reached. Severely retarded children, who have a slower rate of development (but in the same relative sequence), are likely never to develop a complete adult grammar for this reason.

Another consequence is seen in learning a second language:

> The extent of a foreign accent is directly correlated with the age at which the second language is acquired. At the age of three or four practically every child entering a foreign community learns to speak the new language rapidly and without a trace of an accent. This facility declines with age. The proportion of children who speak the second language with an accent tends to increase, but very slowly, so that by the age of 12, perhaps 1% or 2% pronounce words differently from native speakers. A dramatic reversal of form occurs during the early teens, however, when practically every child loses the ability to learn a new language without an accent.[11]

These facts are important for the teacher of English (and of foreign languages), for they indicate that unaccented speech should not be expected of students beyond the elementary years, and overemphasis on precision in pronunciation could lead merely to frustration.

Language is related to concept development.   Given the complexity of language, it is no wonder that even adults with their mature intellects seldom attain native fluency in a new language. But children, with their limited memories, restricted reasoning powers, and as yet almost nonexistent analytical abilities, acquire perfect fluency in any language to which they are consistently exposed, and in which they are motivated to communicate. The ability to acquire language could not be dependent upon intellectual powers alone.

The argument has been discussed above that children universally accomplish this feat because the human infant is genetically endowed with the ability to do so. All available evidence indicates that this ability to acquire a native language is not a function of general intelligence. A twelve-year-old child with an IQ of 50 is in control of a linguistic code.

[10]Brown, *A First Language*, p. 59.

[11]Eric H. Lenneberg, "The Biological Foundation of Language," in *Readings in Applied Transformational Grammar*, pp. 9–11.

His IQ will degenerate to about 30 by the age of twenty, yet he will not lose his linguistic ability.[12] At the same time, a child with a clearly superior IQ will not necessarily begin to speak earlier, or with better results than a child of ordinary intellect.[13] These facts would be difficult to explain, if the ability to acquire language were simply a facet of general intelligence.

Yet language and concept development are inexorably related. There are absolute correspondences between the level of cognitive development and the types of relationships that can be verbalized, and mental age correlates more closely than chronological age with many of the kinds of sentences children understand. We must, of course, question the circularity of these findings. To what extent is measured mental age a construct based on language capability?

Those who work with linguistically diverse children should view with suspicion all claims that the developmental sequence of concepts (such as that posited by Piaget) is universally the same. There is good reason to believe that this sequence is influenced to some extent by the child's cultural experiences.

The sequence of conceptual development may be influenced by the child's native language, since language facilitates (and to some extent may determine) the categorization of experience.[14] Navajo children appear to categorize objects much more frequently along the dimensions of shape and use than do English-speakers of the same age, for instance, and relatively less frequently by color and size. This might be explained by examination of the Navajo language, which requires categorization by shape as a basic grammatical process.

These correlations do not mean that language is entirely *necessary* for cognition. Deaf children organize experience in much the same way as those who hear, and all children can solve many kinds of problems without being able to verbalize them. The reverse is very unlikely; meaningful expression in language can seldom precede cognitive development, although many children can count and repeat symbols for concepts they have not yet acquired.

When a second language is learned by an adult, the process is partly one of learning new labels for concepts that are already developed. (The labels and concepts are almost never entirely identical in two

---

[12]Eric H. Lenneberg, I. A. Nichols, and E. F. Rosenberger, "Primitive Stages of Language Development in Mongolism," in *Disorders of Communication*, Vol. XLII (Research Publications, A.R.N.M.D., 1964), pp 119–37.

[13]Gesell, *The First Five Years of Life*.

[14]Irving E. Segil, "The Attainment of Concepts," in *Review of Child Development Research*, Vol. I, ed. Martin L. Hoffman and Lois Wladis Hoffman (New York: Russell Sage Foundation, 1964).

languages.) In early childhood bilingual contexts, a child is learning to express many new concepts in one language or the other, and language and concept development cannot be separated. This suggests that careful attention should be paid to their developmental sequence in the child's particular culture—for the sake of the child's emotional well-being as well as efficiency.

THE ROLE OF ADULT MODELS, TEACHERS, AND ENVIRONMENT

Children learn to speak.   Not all of language acquisition can be attributed to biological predisposition, for specific learning and stimulus-reinforcement play a definite role. For one thing, a child will never acquire language unless he hears it. Even if the universal properties of language are preprogrammed in the child, he must learn all of those features which distinguish his native language from all other possible human languages. He will learn to speak only the language(s) spoken around him, no matter what his linguistic heritage. An American-born child of Japanese or Greek ancestry will never learn the language of his grandparents if only English surrounds him, and he will find his ancestral language just as hard to learn as any other English-speaker does if he attempts to learn it as an adult. There is no inherent relation between ethnicity and language.

One universal process which children make extensive use of in their language development is analogy, but this process must begin with a model. An English-speaking child hears and uses forms like *cat:cats*; *dog:dogs*; and *book:books*. He unconsciously formulates a generalized rule for English plurals and correctly uses *rats* as the plural of *rat* without ever having heard that particular form before. If his extension to *foots* meets disapproval, he will revise his rule and learn the exception; if he escapes early correction, he will continue to use *foots* until some experience brings the "error" to his attention.

Language is *learned* in the sense that a child cannot acquire it unless he is in an appropriate environment, and in the sense that he will develop whatever specific variety of language (with regard to pronunciation, grammar, and vocabulary) is unique to his social environment.

Adults' language more often follows the model the child sets than vice versa.   They simplify both word choice and grammar, adding more complex structures as the child does, although adults' notion of "simplicity" does not correspond to the actual sequence in language acquisition. Parents imitate their child much more frequently than he imitates them.

In this imitation, adults often provide expansions of the child's utterances. This process is of disputed importance. Brown and Bellugi,[15] Cazden,[16] and Lenneberg[17] would argue that such expansions are not necessary for language learning, and perhaps do not even facilitate it. Others, such as Slobin,[18] think expansions by adults are quite important to linguistic development. Parents' remodeling of children's sentences most probably plays a role in developing at least receptive competence, or the child's ability to understand (but not necessarily produce) new forms.

Children learn more than one style of speech and paralinguistic behavior. Even young children are aware of the changing appropriateness of varied styles of speech in various communicative contexts, and can interpret and use a variety of gestures, facial expressions, and other paralinguistic devices common to their own culture. They frequently engage in role-playing (even when alone, or with or without toys), for instance, adopting different voices for different roles.

Another example is provided by a professor who is from a part of the country where *creek* is pronounced 'crick'; his wife pronounces it 'creak'. When his five-year-old son asked if he could go fishing in the 'creak' one afternoon, the three-year-old daughter corrected him, saying, "Don't you know you're supposed to say 'creak' to Mommy and 'crick' to Daddy?"

Still more supporting examples come from experience in school integration. Children adopt the appropriate pronunciation or usage when they wish to identify with new friends. Anglo children are frequently found adopting the particular English forms of their Black and Spanish-speaking classmates as well as the other way around.

15Roger Brown and Ursula Bellugi, "Three Processes in the Child's Acquisition of Syntax," in *Language and Learning,* special issue of *Harvard Educational Review,* 34 (1964), 133–51.

16Courtney B. Cazden, "Subcultural Differences in Child Language," *Merrill-Palmer Quarterly* 12, no. 3 (1966), 185–219.

17Eric H. Lenneberg, *Biological Foundations of Language* (New York: John Wiley and Sons, 1967); also Lenneberg in *Readings in Applied Transformational Grammar.*

18Dan I. Slobin, "Imitation and Grammatical Development in Children," in *Contemporary Issues in Developmental Psychology,* ed. N. S. Endler, L. R. Boulter, and H. Osser (New York: Holt, Rinehart, and Winston, 1967), pp. 434–37.

Learning is also undoubtedly involved in this aspect of language acquisition and socialization, but there has as yet been no significant research in this area. We can safely assume that the process varies in different linguistic communities, however, and can speculate that it involves:

> Some degree of imitation. There would be cultural differences in who provides the model, in what contexts, and to what extent.
>
> Explicit correction by adults and peers. This is likely to be minimal (again depending on the culture), but occurs whenever someone says, "That's not a nice way to talk," or "Don't look at me like that," or imparts any other rule of sociolinguistic etiquette.
>
> Feedback from social interaction. The reactions of peers to any specific speech styles or behavior, though often unconscious, probably constitute the most potent force in this process.

A study of the body movements of older bilingual children while they were using both languages suggests that a child will use only those characteristics of his native language if it is socially more prestigious, but will tend to modify his gestures and body position when using the second language if it has higher status than his first. When a child's parents each speak a different language natively, this study of French/English bilinguals shows, the child (boy or girl) tends to adopt the paralinguistic system of the mother.[19]

The effects of socioeconomic status are not known. We often hear the claim that economic deprivation and the social conditions associated with it tend to interfere with language development in children. We need to view such claims very skeptically, since in the United States such children are largely from linguistically and culturally "different" groups. Their poor performance on various tests may only be reflective of the linguistic and cultural bias of the tests being used, or of the testing situation, rather than of any deficiency on the part of the children themselves.

However, in spite of its potential hazards to the attitudes and self-concepts of bilingual children, this "deficit" hypothesis is held by many who work with such children. In a handbook for educators published by the Office of Education, for instance, its author states, "The teacher must remember that the child coming from an impoverished environment has had little language development in either his native vernacular or in

---

[19]Reported by Walburga von Raffler Engel in a paper presented to the International Conference on Methods in Dialectology, Charlottetown, P.E.I. (July 1972).

English,"[20] and others have suggested that non-English-speaking children from impoverished groups in the United States must begin learning from scratch because they come to school with no concepts at all!

The latter position may clearly be rejected as misguided and uninformed, but reports on the relation of socioeconomic conditions to language development present us with conflicting evidence.[21] More research urgently needs to be done.

One safe conclusion is that we are not sure what children do *not* know about their language. Another is that both children and languages are exceedingly complex. Part of the disparity in the research results is due to the selective view each investigator takes of what aspect of language to measure: number of words used per sentence, ratio of modifiers to nouns and verbs, percentage of subordinate structures, patterns of word association responses. Tests of language development are not all testing the same thing. Part of the disparity is due to what language subsystem is being selected from; in most cases it is the middle class adult

---

[20]Horacio Ulibarri, *Interpretive Studies on Bilingual Education* (Washington, D.C.: U. S. Office of Education, 1969) , p. 38.

[21]There are research reports which to some extent support the notion of linguistic retardation among children of low socioeconomic status (SES). Pauline A. Jones and William B. McMillan ["Speech Characteristics as a Function of Social Class and Situational Factors," *Child Development*, 44 (1973), 117–21] find the speech of such children to be "less fluent and grammatically less complex," and Nancy Quisenberry ["A Comparison of Vocabulary Diversity and Syntactic Structures in Four-Year-Old Children at Two Socio-Economic Levels" (unpublished doctoral dissertation, Indiana University, 1971)] finds significant lag in their syntactic maturity at age four. Although the lower SES children in these studies tend to be from minority groups in the United States, there is some data from other language communities as well. In a study of Italian children in Rome, Domenico Parisi ["Development of Syntactic Comprehension in Preschool Children as a Function of Socioeconomic Level," *Developmental Psychology*, 5, no. 2, (1971), 186–89] finds that SES differences appear in language development at about three and one-half years and that the split gradually widens, especially between five and one-half and six.

Not all researchers agree. Mildred Templin [*Certain Language Skills in Children: Their Development and Interrelations*, Monographs Series No. 26 (Minneapolis: University of Minnesota, Institute of Child Welfare, 1957)] reports an SES difference in language production at age three, but says there is no indication of cumulative deficit; T. H. Shriner and L. Miner ["Morphological Structures in the Language of Disadvantaged and Advantaged Children," *Journal of Speech and Hearing Research*, 11 no. 3 (1968), 605–10] find no SES differences in children's language structures; and Joyce Evans ["Word-Pair Discrimination and Imitation Abilities of Preschool Economically-Disadvantaged Native-Spanish-Speaking Children," (unpublished doctoral dissertation, University of Texas at Austin, 1971)] finds no SES differences—or Mexican-American versus Anglo differences—in auditory discrimination or repetition tasks. In a fairly extensive study of the language maturity of children in Baltimore and the surrounding area, Doris Entwisle [*Word Associations of Disadvantaged Children* (Baltimore: The Johns Hopkins University, 1956)] found low SES first graders living in slums more advanced linguistically than SES children in the suburbs, although by the third grade the slum children lagged behind.

speech community to which the test-maker or test-giver belongs, and different groups of children will have different degrees of experience with it. Part of the disparity is due to diversity in rapport between child and tester.

We should not deny the importance of language tests because of this complexity, although we should reject the stereotypes which some of them support. These can be very damaging to the self-fulfillment, social development, and educational achievement of many non-English-speaking and bilingual children. In a positive sense, finding out what children *do* know about their language is an important prerequisite to understanding and accepting them where they are, and to using their diverse linguistic and cultural experiences as resources upon which to build.

LEARNING A SECOND LANGUAGE

As a child develops control over his native language, many aspects of perception and production become more and more fixed, and he loses much of the flexibility he had to produce sounds that are not in the language around him. He soon tends to hear all speech sounds in terms of the phonological system of his own language. He does not hear foreign sounds as they are actually produced, but unconsciously pigeonholes them in the categories he has already learned to distinguish for his native language. It is not, for example, that the Spanish speaker is inherently incapable of recognizing the difference between *sh* and *ch*; he has been conditioned *not to* by his experience with his native language, in which the difference between those two sounds is not distinctive and is therefore ignored. The Navajo speaker will have no difficulty perceiving and producing the *sh:ch* distinction in English because it is also made in his native language, but will have difficulty with *k* and *g* (hearing *came* and *game* as homonyms) because they are not distinctive sounds in Navajo. Japanese speakers have difficulty with the English distinction between *l* and *r* for the same reason.

One of the primary steps in learning English as a second language is thus to learn to recognize which differences in sound signal a difference in meaning of English words and to make these differences in speech, at least insofar as intelligibility depends on such distinctions.

Of even greater importance is learning the basic grammatical system of English, the formal features which express meaning or the relationships of elements in sentences. The grammar of one language is never exactly the same as any other, although some closely related languages have many types of structures in common. English, German, French, and

Spanish, for instance, share many grammatical features because they descend from a common ancestral language. Languages such as Navajo, Chinese, and Swahili are completely unrelated, and share only the kinds of grammatical constructs that are common to all language or are similar by chance. The differences in the grammatical systems of two languages often cause problems for students learning a second language. The most critical grammatical features for them to learn in English are word order, derivational and inflectional affixes on words, and such function words as auxiliaries and prepositions, all of which carry a very heavy load in conveying meaning.

Acquiring an adequate vocabulary is the most obviously important need in learning a second language. Practically every word in English has one or more meanings that can be looked up in a dictionary, but vocabulary cannot be learned in grammatical isolation, and students must understand a great deal more than formal definitions of the words they hear if they are to know the full meaning of what an English-speaker says.

To begin with, they must understand the cultural referents which words reflect in English, how such referents are categorized, and even the patterns of thought such linguistic organization represents. An English speaker thinks of *feet* and *back* and *neck* as belonging to all animate creatures, as well as to some inanimate objects such as chairs. The Spanish speaker has learned to consider animals in a different category from humans linguistically, with *patas, lomo,* and *pescuezo* instead of *pies, espalda,* and *cuello.*

The standard box of eight crayons may present another linguistic hurdle because of the different categorization of experience these reflect. The colors considered basic in English do not correspond to the basic color divisions in many other languages. In Navajo, for instance, the blue and green crayons are placed in a single category, labeled *dootł'izh,* whereas English *black* covers two distinct Navajo colors. A teacher of Choctaw children in Oklahoma reported she had thought a child was just "dumb" for coloring a duck brown when he was instructed to color it yellow. But the reason is easy to understand when we realize that these hues are categorized together under a single term meaning "earth color" in Muskogean languages.

Gestures, intonation, and even facial expressions that accompany language are very important to understanding what someone says, and these, too, are different in different language communities. The normal voice level in English may be interpreted as anger by a child from another language background, and that child's respectful aversion of his eyes may be interpreted as shyness or sneakiness by the English-speaker.

Smiling at a stranger may receive varying interpretations from "friendly" to "wicked," even from region to region in the United States.

The question of what contributes to meaning is of considerable current interest to linguistic theoreticians, and much of what they have to say is relevant to those concerned with second language learning. The meaning of what is said, for instance, is largely dependent on what is *not* said, on what is presupposed or implied. Because misunderstandings at this level of interpretation are seldom expressed, we often fail to recognize them. We can be sure, however, that problems in this area are common for anyone learning English as a second language.

First and second language acquisition are analogous in many respects. Recognizing this, our second language methodology has tried to replicate the conditions which were thought to be present when the first language is learned, but such attempts have been largely unsuccessful, partly because of misconceptions about first language learning and partly because the methods used were developed with adults and transferred without adequate adaptation to younger students. Of course, first and second language acquisition cannot really be the same process, because the second language is filtered through the first and will be partially modified by it. Additionally, students have already learned how to communicate verbally when they approach a second language, and are cognitively more advanced. Beyond these inherent restrictions, our methodology has not recognized or taken into account the similarities that do exist between the two processes.

We know, for instance, that first language acquisition is not essentially habit formation but inductive generalization and hypothesis testing in a variety of communication contexts. The child learning his first language "naturally" communicates with adults or other children about topics of direct immediate relevance to him. His departures from adult norms are not perceived as mistakes, but as developmental stages in language learning, and are seldom directly "corrected" by adults, and rarely by peers. He understands the language around him because of its meaningful context, and in a gradual and natural sequence that accompanies biological and cognitive growth.

Methodology based on what we know about child language acquisition will:

Minimize the role of rote memorization and meaningless drill

Introduce second language data, including drill practice, only in meaningful contexts

Maximize the positive transfer of what is known in the first language to the second, and minimize interference between the two systems

Develop classroom communication situations to allow for hypothesis formation and testing by students

Provide maximum need and opportunity for children to use their second
language in communicating with adults and peers concerning things which
are relevant and interesting to them

Not all children learn a second language the same way or for the
same reasons. There are first of all four basic circumstances under which
children acquire English as a second language: two languages may be
spoken at home; the first language may be spoken at home and English
used exclusively for school and with a few out-of-school peers; one or
both languages may be spoken at home and both at school in a bilingual
program; or one language may be spoken at home and school with
English encountered only as a foreign language.

Children who learn two languages at home often develop the competence to operate independently in either language system, or become
coordinate bilinguals. They may also become *integrated* bilinguals if
they live in a bilingual community and learn *code-switching,* a phenom-
enon in which a speaker can switch from one language to the other at
will and in accordance with appropriate contexts. This is a systematic
and rule-governed linguistic process which is described in more detail
in the following chapter.

A child who learns English at school but always speaks another
language at home may also become a *coordinate* bilingual, but his two
language systems may have very little area of overlap. He will seldom
have occasion to discuss the topics concerning home in English, and the
school subjects may rarely be mentioned in his home language. This
creates a division of *domains* in language competence called *diglossia,*
which probably minimizes interference between the two languages for
bilinguals, although it also creates some limitations. Many bilingual
teachers schooled in the United States, for instance, have difficulty using
their native language to instruct students in subjects which they
themselves have only studied in English. This limitation is soon overcome with practice, however, once the necessary vocabulary for the subject has been learned in the native language.

The child from a non-English-speaking background who is in a
bilingual program has several apparent advantages over one who must
operate in English alone at school. He can communicate with his peers
and with adults as he did before coming to school, his cognitive development continues in an unbroken sequence, and he can learn initial reading
and writing skills in a language he already knows without being retarded
by needing to learn English before any other learning can continue. An

apparent disadvantage is the reduction of need and opportunity to speak English in a society which requires this competence for success and mobility. This potential limitation need not retard learning, however, if appropriate English as a second language (ESL) methods and materials are used.

The child who learns English as a foreign language in another country and never *needs* to use it for communicative purposes is least likely to become fluent in it, is most likely to continue a translation process through his native language when using the foreign language, and is most likely to experience misunderstanding when a need for communication does arise.

Within any one of these basic circumstances for learning English as a second language, children will have different styles of learning, levels of ability, and foci of interest. Even an entire class of students labeled disadvantaged will exhibit a full range of abilities, when they are provided with a full range of educational opportunities. The term "disadvantaged" came into use during the 1960s as a rather unfortunate label for any children who lacked the economic and supposed cultural blessings, hence "advantages," of the middle class mainstream of American society. At best, the term is a euphemism for poor, lower class, or "underprivileged," at worst a culturally biased viewpoint of desirable norms of values and behavior. Since low-income groups are heavily populated by ethnic minorities, the term "disadvantaged" therefore includes many students who are from non-English-speaking backgrounds. It is significant, however, that foreign students, or the children of foreign scholars and diplomats, seldom find that a lack of fluency in English alone constitutes a major barrier to success in our school systems.

Providing for "advantaged" students in a class may be as challenging to a teacher as providing for the "disadvantaged." When the toy shelves at home are overflowing with puzzles, games, and chemistry sets, and when numbers and letters dance across the family's television screen, it is often difficult to capture a child's interest with less attractive educational trappings in the classroom.

Both slow learners and gifted students will be found in both the so-called disadvantaged and the so-called advantaged groups, and the eagerness of the gifted child to learn is no less fragile and in need of careful nurture than the slower learner's self-concept and willingness to try.

The range of individual differences across these groups include differences in:

> Starting points. Students do not enter any class with identical experiences or equal proficiency.

Learning rates. Students who start at a lower level in their English competence are not necessarily slower learners, and the pace of learning does not remain constant for most children. It can change radically with either good or poor teaching.

Motivation. Students will have different values and different goals, and greater or lesser desire to succeed in school.

Interests. Students will enjoy different topics and choose to pursue different activities.

Learning-styles. Some students learn best by trial-and-error involvement in learning, others by passive observation; some learn best from an adult teacher, others from peer group members.

Coping-styles. Students face problem situations in the classroom (including challenging learning tasks) in a variety of ways. Some are competitive, some cooperative, some defeatist, and some hostile. Some ask for help, while others are self-reliant.

Needs. The same content will not be relevant for all students.

We must approach methods of teaching both English and other content subjects through the medium of English as a second language with these differences in mind and add to them a consideration of the diverse social influences on second language learning and use.

FOR ADDITIONAL READING

BAR-ADON, AARON and WERNER F. LEOPOLD, eds., *Child Language: A Book of Readings* (Englewood Cliffs, N.J.: Prentice-Hall, Inc., 1971) .

BLOOM, LOIS, *Language Development* (Cambridge, Mass.: The M.I.T. Press, 1975) .

CAZDEN, COURTNEY B., *Child Language and Education* (New York: Holt, Rinehart and Winston, 1972) .

ERVIN-TRIPP, SUSAN, *Becoming a Bilingual*, ERIC No. ED 018 786 (1968) .

FERGUSON, CHARLES A. and DAN I. SLOBIN, eds., *Studies of Child Language Development* (New York: Holt, Rinehart and Winston, 1973) .

FISHMAN, JOSHUA A., ed., *Readings in the Sociology of Language* (The Hague: Mouton, 1968), especially Section V: "Multilingualism," pp. 473–584.

HALLIDAY, M. A. K., *Learning How to Mean: Explorations in the Development of Language* (London: Edward Arnold, 1975) .

JAKOBOVITS, LEON A. and M. S. MIRON, *Readings in the Psychology of Language* (Englewood Cliffs, N.J.: Prentice-Hall, Inc., 1967) .

LUGTON, ROBERT C., ed., *Toward a Cognitive Approach to Second Language Acquisition* (Philadelphia, Pa.: The Center for Curriculum Development, 1971).

MACNAMARA, JOHN, ed., "Problems of Bilingualism," *The Journal of Social Issues,* 23 (1967).

PIMSLEUR, PAUL and TERENCE QUINN, *The Psychology of Second Language Learning,* Papers from the Second International Congress of Applied Linguistics, Cambridge, 8–12 Sept. 1969. (Cambridge: Cambridge University Press, 1971).

REED, CARROLL E., ed., *The Learning of Language* (New York: Appleton-Century-Crofts, 1971).

ROSENTHALL, ROBERT and LEONORE JACOBSON, *Pygmalion in the Classroom: Teacher Expectation and Pupils' Intellectual Development* (New York: Holt, Rinehart and Winston, 1968).

SAPORTA, SOL, ed., *Psycholinguistics: A Book of Readings* (New York: Holt, Rinehart and Winston, 1961).

SLOBIN, DAN I., "Children and Language: They Learn the Same Way All Around the World," *Psychology Today,* 6, no. 2 (1972), 71–74, 82.

SMITH, FRANK and G. A. MILLER, *The Genesis of Language: A Psycholinguistic Approach* (Cambridge, Mass.: The M.I.T. Press, 1966).

Linguistic Foundations

CHAPTER 3

THE NATURE OF LANGUAGE

What is it that a child is learning when he acquires one or more languages? Definitions of language usually refer to its verbal features (oral and written), to its function in communication, and to its uniquely human character, but as a foundation for teaching language, we require a much deeper understanding of its complex nature and use. It will be helpful to begin with a consideration of some of the most salient facts about language which we have learned from the field of linguistics.

The spoken form of language is basic.   Speech ocurred long before writing in the history of language, as it does in the language development of every child. Even today writing is far from a universal characteristic of language: of the more than three thousand languages spoken in the world, fewer than half have ever been represented in writing. Writing is a cultural invention, the existence or absence of which has little effect on the basic nature of a language. Unwritten languages are not less complicated or sophisticated than written ones.

Language is systematic.   It consists of recurrent elements which occur in regular patterns of relationships. Each variety (or dialect) of a language is a slightly different system, but equally regular. The vast majority of all sentences which are used have not been memorized, but are created according to a system of rules which the speaker is usually unconscious of using—or of even knowing—if he acquired the language as a young child. It is safe to assume, for instance, that most of the sentences in a daily newspaper are combinations of words that have never been used before, because most of the events being reported have never occurred before. These new sentences are understandable because we understand the principles (the *system*) by which the words are combined to express meanings.

Language is symbolic. Language is a type of code. Experience is encoded by the speaker, transmitted by speech, and decoded by the hearer. There is no resemblance between the four-legged animal that eats hay and the spoken symbols [*hors*] or the written symbols *horse* which we use to represent it in English.

No sequences of sounds or letters inherently possess meaning. The meanings of symbols in a language comes through the agreement of a group of speakers. English-speakers agree that the hay-eating animal will be called *horse,* Spanish-speakers *caballo,* German *Pferd,* Chinese *ma,* Turks *at,* and Navajos *łį́į́'.*

We sometimes feel that onomatapoetic words do possess meaning in themselves and are not arbitrary symbols, but the *bow-wow* of a dog belonging to an English speaker is *amh-amh* in Irish, *av-av* in Serbo-Croatian, and *wang-wang* in Chinese. It makes no difference whether the dog is an Irish setter or a Pekinese. Kindergarten and primary teachers know that children must be taught the English terms for animal noises when they teach "Old MacDonald Had a Farm." Children realistically imitate animals they have heard before they learn *oink, neigh,* or the conventional terms in any language.

Languages change. The process of change in language is slow, but inevitable unless all of the speakers of the language are dead. Misguided efforts to "preserve" the language forms of today or yesterday are futile and unfounded. Modern French is merely a changed form of Latin, and no one suggests that the Frenchman of today has any more difficulty communicating than did his Roman ancestor.

Language is social. The nature and form of each language reflects the social requirements of the society that uses it, and there is no standard for judging the effectiveness of a language other than to estimate its success in achieving the social tasks that are demanded of it. Although the capacity for language is inherent in the neurological makeup of every individual, no one can develop that potential without interaction with others in a society. We use language to communicate, to categorize and catalogue the objects, events, and processes of human experience. We might well define language as "the expressive dimension of culture."

It follows that a person who functions in more than one cultural context will communicate more effectively if he has access to more than one language or variety of a language.

Language is variable. Every person has unique linguistic experiences and speaks in a way slightly different from the way anyone else speaks. This unique individual speech pattern is called an *idiolect*. The idiolects of a group of people who are in frequent communication from childhood on will be very similar, and will differ from the idiolects of other groups of speakers with whom they have little contact. A group of similar idiolects which differs from others in some aspects of pronunciation, grammar, or vocabulary is called a *variety,* either social or regional. Groups of similar varieties compose a language. All languages have varieties, and every speaker of a language is a speaker of a variety of that language.

This means that there is no such thing as a "pure" language. All regional and social varieties of a language are equally well developed and systematic. They are *not* the results of imperfect attempts to emulate the "pure" or "real" language. Each child who is born into a language community learns to speak the variety spoken by those people with whom he is in consistent contact in his early years.

LANGUAGE VARIETY

Language varieties come about as the result of natural processes of change in the pronunciation, grammar, and vocabulary of people who are geographically or socially separated from one another. Linguistic divergence is a gradual and cumulative process, with small initial differences becoming marked variations the longer and more completely the groups remain separated.

Many such changes begin as differences between the speech of adults and children. Most are "corrected" to some extent, either directly or by adult example. In almost all respects, children speak the language of their parents. As children come together in play groups, however, peer group pressure and the prestige of individuals in the group lead to the emergence of group norms of usage, and groups of children who are isolated from one another by distance or social barriers will often develop slightly different linguistic systems. This is one of the basic agents of change in language.

To illustrate regional differences in vocabulary and pronunciation, a child who learns to speak English in Boston, Massachusetts, will carry water in a *pail,* but a child learning English in Austin, Texas, will use a *bucket.* A child learning English in most of the southern United States will not make a distinction in the pronunciations of *pin* and *pen,* but will pronounce *cot* and *caught* differently; a child in California will distinguish between *pin* and *pen,* but not *cot* and *caught.* A host of similar lexical and phonological examples can be found, but almost no grammatical differences in English have exclusive regional distribution.

Groups of speakers separated by social barriers also quite naturally develop slightly different norms in usage, called *social varieties.* This term usually refers to division along socioeconomic lines, but groups of speakers isolated for religious reasons (as the Amish) also speak their own variety of English. There may be marked generational differences between the older and younger members of a speech community in addition to those which arise in the course of initial language acquisition, and the speech of men and of women differ in several ways. A man admiring another man's new head covering would probably never exclaim, "What an exquisite hat!"

A recent comparison of the spontaneous speaking vocabulary of four- to six-year-old "disadvantaged" children in Missouri and generally middle class kindergarten children in New England shows extensive regional and social differences.[1] The lower class children used words like *chitlins, skillet, lingo, shoats* 'poor people', *pokey, greens,* and *fetch* (several of these words are also used by even the higher socioeconomic levels in the South), but they used no words at all in the bird and plant categories collected in New England. The lower class children used such words as *apron, vegetable,* and *party* with much less frequency than middle class children, and *rat, trash, steal,* and *whip* much more. Such differences in language use quite obviously reflect wide differences in cultural experiences, and in what the children will find understandable, relevant, or interesting.

Not all Spanish-speaking children have the same language system any more than all English-speaking children do, not even all those who live in the United States. Many have come with their families from Cuba,

---

[1]John K. Sherk, *A Word-Count of Spoken English of Culturally Disadvantaged Preschool and Elementary Pupils* (Kansas City: University of Missouri, 1973).

Puerto Rico, or various parts of Mexico or South America. Many others are members of families who have lived for generations in parts of the United States where regional varieties of Spanish have continued to develop and change. All of these regional dialects have, as does English, stratified social varieties, creating the kind of complex language diversity that inevitably accompanies the geographical and social dispersion of its speakers.

The Spanish-speaking child will learn to pronounce *calle* as [kalye] in Peru, [kaye] in Mexico, and [kae] in parts of Texas and the Southwest. He will ride downtown on a *camión* in Mexico, *guagua* in Puerto Rico, *camioneta* in Guatemala, and *omnibus* through South America. Extensive differences are also to be found between the French of children in Louisiana and Maine, the Chinese of children in California and New York, and the Polish of children in Texas and Massachusetts. Variation in these languages, as well as in English, reflects both geographic and social distance between groups.

No variety of a language is inherently better than any other. Judgments on the relative "value" of different varieties are made purely on social, economic, and political grounds, and have nothing to do with the linguistic qualities of the varieties themselves. The varieties of upper class, educated speakers come to be judged "standard" in most literate societies and are used as the basis for written language, while the varieties of less prestigious speakers come to be considered "nonstandard."

The recognition and acceptance of linguistic diversity is critical in educational programs because any approach which stigmatizes a child's speech (or that of his family) will probably humiliate him, and certainly will create an environment which is not conducive to learning. There are additional important implications for later education since the child's own variety of his native language may affect the nature of the problems he will have in learning such secondary linguistic skills as reading and spelling, and the specific problems he will have in learning English as a second language.

GRAMMAR

The most familiar unit in English is the *word*, and *grammar* has to do with the way words are formed and how they in turn go together to make up phrases and sentences. These two grammatical processes are often labeled separately as *morphology* and *syntax*.

The smallest unit of meaning in any language is called a *morpheme*, and every word in English is made up of one or more of them. *Cat* is a single morpheme, meaning 'animal with whiskers that meows'; *cats* is two morphemes, *cat* plus another unit *-s* which means 'more than one'. *Walk* is a single morpheme; *walked* is two, *walk* plus *-ed* meaning 'past'. The basic morpheme which carries most of the meaning is called a *base*, and morphemes added on to modify that meaning are called *affixes* (they may be either prefixes or suffixes).

Some English words are very complex, such as *antidisestablishmentarianism*, which contains a base *establish* and six affixes: *anti-, dis-, -ment, -ar, -ian,* and *-ism,* each a separate morpheme. While no child needs to learn such complex English forms, there is a basic set of grammatically important affixes that should be taught to every student learning English as a second language.

With nouns
 -s plural
 -'s possessive
With adjectives
 -er comparative
 -est superlative
With verbs
 -s third person singular, present tense
 -ed past
 -ing present participle
 -en past participle[2]

Many of us have learned the verb inflections in other languages through "conjugation" drills, but a comparison of English and Spanish forms for *hablar* 'to speak' should illustrate what a waste of time it would be for our students to learn to conjugate verbs in English.

Present

	Singular		Plural	
	hablo	'speak'	*hablamos*	'speak'
	hablas	'speak'	*habláis*	'speak'
	habla	'speaks'	*hablan*	'speak'

Past

	Singular		Plural	
	hable	'spoke'	*hablamos*	'spoke'
	hablaste	'spoke'	*hablasteis*	'spoke'
	hable	'spoke'	*hablaron*	'spoke'

[2]These morphemes have been listed in their most common shape, but individual words will have alternate forms or irregular shapes.

A complete account of the present and past tenses in Spanish requires six different verb forms each, because there *are* six forms. English has only two in the present, *speak* and *speaks,* and one in the past. Borrowing the practice of conjugating verbs from Spanish, French, or Latin is therefore both misleading and of little benefit in developing a child's control over the verb system of English.

The five verb forms which are used in English are illustrated by the following sentences:

> They *speak* Spanish.
> He also *speaks* French.
> He *spoke* to the principal.
> I am *speaking* to the PTA.
> Mary has *spoken* of you often.

All of the tense and aspect possibilities in English are made with one of these five verb forms and a helping verb *(be* or *have)*:

> Present
>   "simple"   *(talk/talks)*
>   progressive   *(is/are talking)*
>   perfect   *(has/have talked)*
>   passive   *(is being talked)*
> Past
>   "simple"   *(talked)*
>   progressive   *(was talking)*
>   perfect   *(had talked)*
>   present perfect progressive   *(have been talking)*
>   past perfect progressive   *(had been talking)*
>   passive   *(has been talked)*
> Future
>   "simple"   *(will talk)*
>   progressive   *(will be talking)*
>   perfect   *(will have talked)*
>   future perfect progressive   *(will have been talking)*
>   passive   *(will have been talked)*

Other common affixes are used to derive nouns, adjectives, or verbs from other parts of speech. Students must learn how to use these derivational processes if they are to create grammatical sentences of any length; knowing even a few of these affixes will greatly extend their basic vocabulary:

Derived nouns
   Add -*ness* to adjectives   *(happiness)*
   Add -*er* to verbs   *(dancer)*
Derived adjectives
   Add -*ful* or -*ous* to nouns   *(joyful; joyous)*
   Add -*ish* to nouns   *(kittenish)*
Derived verbs
   Add -*ing* or -*ed* to nouns   *(singing; crated)*

Some of the other morphemes which carry a heavy grammatical load and must therefore be taught early in an ESL program are:

Pronouns
   Personal   *(I, you, he, . . .)*
   Relative   *(that, which, who)*
   Demonstrative   *(this, that, these, those)*
Prepositions   *(in, on, at, . . .)*
Auxiliaries   *(be, do, have)*
Question words   *(how, when, where, . . .)*
Articles   *(a, the)*
Negatives   *(no, not, none)*

A speaker of any language will already know that words are seldom independent entities, but occur in a grammatical framework. Two of the most important aspects of this framework in English are the relative order of words and their agreement with one another.

Although a number of different sequences of word order are found in English, they normally follow consistent structural patterns which have either grammatical or stylistic significance. In many cases, as illustrated in the following pairs of sentences, a change of word order will completely change the meaning:

Bill hit John.   John hit Bill.
Naturally he answered.   He answered naturally.
He is standing still.   He is still standing.
We have a guest house.   We have a house guest.

When native speakers of English are asked to collapse sentences with several adverbs or adjectives into a single structure, there is seldom any disagreement about the word order.

I am going
+ *I am going home*
+ *I am going at 5:00*

+ *I am going by car*
    = *I am going home by car at 5:00*
                (place + manner + time)

I bought shoes
+ *The shoes are old*
+ *The shoes are leather*
+ *There are ten shoes*
+ *I bought those shoes*
        = *I bought those ten old leather shoes*
            (determiner + number + age + material)

Native speakers of English are often surprised to discover that they "know" how to put the words in this order so automatically since they have seldom been consciously taught anything about this order, but it is a part of English grammar and must be taught to someone who is learning English as a second language.

Agreement in English refers both to grammatical form and to choice of what must occur together. For example, a verb in the present tense is said to *agree* in number with its subject: a third person requires an *-s* form of the verb; plural subjects require *are.* Singular countable nouns occur with the determiner *a* while plural ones do not; *any* occurs only in questions or with negatives, *some* is the affirmative form. In addition, English permits certain verbs to omit their objects, allowing *The horse ate* but not **John found.* (The asterisk before a sentence indicates that it is not a sentence of English—that it is ungrammatical.) Others must be followed by some element which completes them, so we normally say *I said I would go* but not just **I said.* Thus in learning a new word, it is necessary to learn much more than just its meaning, for all of the restrictions on its use must be learned also. Unless they are, we cannot say that the word is really learned.

The basic sentence patterns which students need to learn are:

Equational
    This is a pencil.   (NP   *be*   NP)
    Jane is sick.   (NP   *be*   Adj)
    Joe is in the office.   (NP   *be*   Adv)
Intransitive
    He is walking.   (NP   Aux V_i)
    John runs fast.   (NP V_i Adv)
Transitive
    Bill kicked the dog.   (NP_1 V_t NP_2)
    Mary bought an ice cream cone.   (NP_1 V_t NP_2)

Pete gave the ball to him/Pete gave him the ball.
$(NP_1 \quad V_t \quad NP_2 \quad to \quad NP_3 \quad / \quad NP_1 \quad V_t \quad NP_3 \quad NP_2)$

Students should also be able to perform a few *transformations* on these basic structures, in order to:

Join nouns, adjectives, verbs, and sentences with *and*.
Change a statement into a question.
Change a statement into a command.
Change an affirmative statement into a negative one.
Use reflexive pronouns in simple sentences.

In no case is it necessary for students to learn *about* English grammar in ESL, but only to *understand* and to *use* the structures that have been listed here.

PHONOLOGY

Every language (and variety of a language) uses a limited number of classes of sounds to signal the differences between words. The number of such distinctive sounds, called *phonemes,* ranges from as few as sixteen (in Hawaiian) to sixty (in Circassian, a Caucasian language), with English standing about halfway between these extremes.

A student of any age learning English must learn to hear, and then produce, twenty-four distinctive consonant sounds. The symbol used for each of these phonemes is enclosed in slanted lines (/ /), and is sometimes different from the symbol which represents the sound in conventional spelling. Some sounds in English are spelled in several ways, as the /f/ sound in *f*ear, *ph*oto, and enou*gh*. The system of notation used here allows one symbol to consistently represent one distinctive sound.

These consonant phonemes are classified according to the way they are pronounced, as *stops, affricates, fricatives* (sometimes called *spirants*), *resonants,* and *nasals.* In the chart on the next page, each phoneme is illustrated by an example in the conventional spelling system.

Vowel sounds are classified according to where they are produced in the mouth, as *high, mid,* or *low,* and according to which part of the tongue is active in their articulation, as *front, central,* or *back.* In addition, some English vowels are further distinguished according to whether the tongue is *tense* or *lax* in their production. Tense vowels in English

Consonants of English

		Voiceless		Voiced	
Stops					
	Sounds produced by complete closing of the passage of air through the mouth	/p/	pie	/b/	boy
		/t/	tie	/d/	dog
		/k/	cat	/g/	gate
Affricates					
	Stop consonants released with a friction sound	/č/	chair	/ǰ/	giant
Fricatives					
	Produced by a constriction causing friction in the mouth but not completely closing the air passage	/f/	fair	/v/	very
		/θ/	thing	/ð/	this
		/s/	sit	/z/	zebra
		/š/	shell	/ž/	azure
		/h/	house		
Resonants					
	Produced without friction; /w/ and /y/ are often called semivowels or glides			/w/	wash
				/y/	yellow
				/l/	light
				/r/	rat
Nasals					
	Produced with the stream of air flowing through the nasal passage rather than through the mouth			/m/	man
				/n/	name
				/ŋ/	sing

are usually pronounced with a /y/-glide (if the vowel is front) or a /w/-glide (if the vowel is back).

The following are distinctive vowel sounds in most regional varieties of American English:

Vowels of English

		Front		Central		Back	
High	(Tense)	/i/	beet			/u/	boot
	(Lax)	/ɪ/	bit			/u/	book
Mid	(Tense)	/e/	bait	/ə/	but*	/o/	boat
	(Lax)	/ɛ/	bet				
Low		/æ/	bat	/a/	cot	/ɔ/	caught†

*The vowel of *but* is also written /ʌ/.

†In many northern and western varieties of American English, /ɔ/ is not distinguished from /a/; a single intermediate vowel is often used.

The phonemes of a language can be identified by finding pairs of words that differ in only one sound, and yet have different meanings. One such *minimal* pair in English is /dɛn/ *den* and /tɛn/ *ten*. Because the /d/ and /t/ signal a difference in meaning, they indicate that /d/ and /t/ are contrastive phonemes in the English sound system. The pair /θɪŋ/ *thing* and /sɪŋ/ *sing* contrast /θ/ and /s/, and /bɪn/ *bin* and /bin/ *bean* prove the distinctiveness of the vowels /ɪ/ and /i/.

A single phoneme, such as /k/, may be articulated quite differently in different words. For instance, the /k/ of *key* is articulated farther front than the /k/ of *cough*. The difference between these two sounds makes no difference in meaning to the English speaker, however, so the variants are not considered separate phonemes. It is quite probable that the native speaker of English will never even notice the difference unless it is called to his attention. Linguists call these phonetic variants of phonemes *allophones*. Sounds that are allophones in one language may be phonemes (i.e., sounds that make a difference in meaning) in another; for example, the difference between the /k/ of *kill* and *skill* (note the puff of air in *kill* would make a difference in meaning in Hindi).

VOCABULARY

It was noted above that every word in a language has one or more meanings that can be looked up in a dictionary, but that we must understand a great deal more than that to know the meaning of what someone actually says.

The *denotative meaning,* the concept or experience the word refers to, is certainly basic. The *connotative meaning,* or the feelings and attitudes attached to a word by a native speaker is far more difficult for anyone from another culture to learn, and the *presuppositions,* or usually unconscious assumptions and information shared by the speakers and never explicitly stated, are most difficult of all for learners of a second language. To add to a student's confusion, the rules of meaning we operate by in natural communication settings are sometimes violated in a classroom context. For instance, when someone asks a question like *How many brothers do you have?*, the speaker presupposes that the hearer has some brothers, and the hearer may presuppose that the speaker doesn't know how many. But an adult may ask a child *How many eyes do you have?* when it is quite obvious to both that he already knows the answer. Such violations of the normal rules of language use are quite common when teachers talk to children, and may partially explain why some groups of children often do not respond well to such test items.

An unknown number of misunderstandings, of misinterpretations, of misjudgments, occur for this reason across languages, between generations, and between different ethnic and socioeconomic groups—and we are seldom even aware when there has been a problem.

Deciding which small portion of the vocabulary students with limited facility in English need to know is an important consideration. There are hundreds of thousands of words in the language, and our students may never learn (or need) more than two or three percent of these. Beyond a very limited list of high frequency items that carry a heavy load of grammatical information (prepositions, conjunctions, *be, have, do,* pronouns, determiners), the occurrence of specific words depends largely on the context in which the student finds himself. A student who speaks English in his city home may have frequent use for terms for buildings, streets, and objects in the supermarket. A student of the same age who speaks English on his family's farm will use terms for animals, plants, farm machinery, and often know words for cloud formations or types of air movement or precipitation. Both will know and use English terms for relatives, household furniture, and kitchen utensils. The student who speaks English only at school would find little need for household words and kinship terms, but must include in his limited English vocabulary words and expressions needed to follow directions in class, ask for the supplies he wants, get home on the school bus, order food in the cafeteria, and understand the content of whatever subjects he is being presented in English. This is a very large order for students just beginning in a monolingual program, and one that requires careful organization and sequencing of material.

Primary criteria for the selection of vocabulary for auxiliary or support instruction in English should be the students' need to know the words, the opportunities the students will have to use and repeat them, and the extent to which the students are or can be interested in the words' referents—their relevance.

These are criteria which the vocabulary selection of no commercially available ESL material can completely satisfy for specific students in specific contexts. Fully relevant content in a language that is needed as a medium for learning must be selected, arranged in sequence, and taught by educators within that context who are sensitive to their students' specific needs, opportunities, and interests. To repeat, one of the primary considerations in vocabulary selection is the content vocabulary of whatever subjects are being studied in English. The need to know these words is readily apparent, opportunities to use and repeat them are built into the content lessons, and interest in any subject will surely be enhanced by better understanding of the language which conveys it.

CONTRASTING LANGUAGES

For the last thirty years, most linguists have been approaching the topic of the interaction of languages in education from a contrastive point of view. That is, they first compare the native language of the students with the second language of instruction in order to describe the structural differences between them, predict which elements of the second language will be most troublesome for students from a particular language background, and then order these troublesome elements for systematic and efficient instruction. Techniques and models for such contrastive analyses differ widely today, and even greater divergence can be expected as more aspects of current linguistic theory are incorporated into language teaching contexts.

The contrastive approach tries to identify and account for the ways in which the speech patterns of a student's native language interfere with his acquisition of second language speech patterns. Where patterns (of sounds, grammar, or vocabulary) in the two languages are similar, a student should have little interference from his native language and should find those elements of the second language relatively easy to learn. Where patterns are completely dissimilar, the new element may not be perceived accurately and the closest native language form used in its place. Where patterns are partially similar, as words which have similar form but different meanings (so-called false friends or false cognates, for example, Spanish *asistir* and English *assist*), even greater interference might be predicted for the learner.

The value of the contrastive approach in identifying interference phenomena has been debated recently by many linguists. Interference does not always occur where it is predicted, and unpredictable problems appear, so that a knowledge of the differences between language structures should be supplemented by a careful compilation and study of the actual deviations made by the students. Nevertheless, the teacher's perception can be greatly aided by knowing in advance what kinds of difficulties the students may have, and *why*. Such predictive information also assists in advance planning, selection, and preparation of materials, and in the construction of efficient tests for speakers from different language backgrounds.

One area of interlinguistic interference is grammar. The grammatical system of a language includes all of the formal features which express meaning or the relationships of elements in sentences. The grammar of one language is different from any other, although some closely related languages have many types of structures in common. English and Spanish will share many more grammatical features than, say, English and Navajo because English and Spanish descend from a common ancestral language, whereas English and Navajo do not.

The contrast between the word order of Spanish and English may be seen in this example:

> *Es un hombre.*   '*He is a man.*'

Such contrast in word order explains why some speakers of Spanish when learning English produce such sentences as *Is a man,* following the Spanish sentence pattern. The carry-over of English word order to Spanish explains such constructions as *Mi papa's carro* for *El carro de mi papá.*

Other common points of potential grammatical interference are prepositions, pronouns, and agreement of subject and verb or adjective.

A typical example of phonological interference in English for speakers of Spanish is the *sh:ch* distinction, as in *share* versus *chair* or *washing* versus *watching.* The most interesting questions on this topic, however, are about the importance of such "mistakes."

A great deal of emphasis has been placed in the past on the accurate pronunciation of a second language, and instructional priority has frequently been given to hour upon hour of often meaningless repetition drill in the hope of reaching this goal. It was maintained that *complete* mastery of the sound system was essential, with vocabulary acquisition of much lesser importance.

This priority cannot be justified by the realities of communication or by student needs, at least in English as a second language. English tolerates a great deal of variety in pronunciation while remaining intelligible, undoubtedly in part because of its high degree of redundancy. There are few if any pairs of words distinguished only by *sh* or *ch* that would be misunderstood in context, and the infrequent pairs which might occur in the same place in a sentence (such as *pin* and *pen,* which are homophones for many English-speakers) are disambiguated by further modification (as in *Give me a stick pin* versus *Give me an ink pen*).

The relative importance of accurate pronunciation in any language must be judged by social criteria as well as intelligibility, however, because pronunciation is probably the most obvious clue to social group membership. Both speakers and listeners often attach strong feelings to the information it may convey.

A foreign "accent" may be prestigious (if it is French, Hungarian, or symbolic of another group we hold in high regard), but it has historically been a handicap to members of less prestigious groups in the United States because it has been used consciously or unconsciously as a vehicle of prejudice. Although we can see a trend toward more tolerance of linguistic diversity, particularly with the spread of bilingual education, it is clear that such biases still exist.

Cultural identity may also be at stake for the speaker as well as the perceiver, and must also be taken into account. A person who wishes to retain his native cultural identity and not identify with an English-speaking social group has no reason to "perfect" his English pronunciation. He may have good reason *not* to. Indeed, if he is foreign-born, it may be to his advantage to retain an "accent," since this signals to a native speaker that he controls the language less than perfectly, and gives him greater latitude to deviate from native usage.

LANGUAGE IN USE

Besides sharing common features of vocabulary, pronunciation, and grammar, each speech community shares a set of values regarding the uses of language in various contexts. These include judgments on the relative prestige of different regional and social varieties, group and role identifications, and feelings about the appropriateness of different styles of language for self-expression on different occasions.

Some of our rules for language use vary systematically depending on the social contexts of the speech act. These may trigger changes in our pronunciation, grammar, choice of words, gestures, and all other aspects of our linguistic behavior. A speaker's ability to interpret and produce appropriate styles of a language are part of his total communicative competence. The components of the social context that must be considered conveniently form the acronym SPEAKING:[4]

[4]This acronym is suggested as a mnemonic device by Dell Hymes in "Models of the Interaction of Language and Social Life," *Directions in Sociolinguistics: The Ethnography of Communication,* ed. John Gumperz and Dell Hymes (New York: Holt, Rinehart and Winston, 1972), p. 59.

Setting

Where and when the speech act is taking place. Children are generally allowed to be louder outdoors than in, for instance, and may have learned they are supposed to whisper (or not talk at all) in church.

Participants

Age, sex, kinship, social class, education, or occupation may make a difference. An English-speaker would seldom have difficulty identifying the listener in a conversation as a young child by the speaker's grammar, word choice, and intonation (although the same style is sometimes used with pets). Many languages have different pronominal forms to indicate social distance, and the sex of a speaker to some extent determines appropriate word choice.

Ends

Style sometimes depends on purpose: is the speech act a request, demand, query, warning, or mere statement of information?

Act sequence

This refers to the prescribed form a speech act takes when it is closely controlled by the culture, as is usually the case with prayers, public speeches or lectures, and classroom interaction. It also refers to what may be talked about in each, what can be appropriately prayed about versus what can be appropriately joked about.

Key

The same words may express various tones, moods, or manners (serious, playful, belligerent, sarcastic). The signal may be nonverbal, such as a wink or gesture, or conveyed by intonation, word choice, or some other linguistic convention.

Instrumentalities

Different verbal codes may be selected. A bilingual may choose between languages, and even a monolingual will have a choice of registers (varieties along a formal–informal continuum). Many speakers are able to choose among regional and social varieties as well. The choice is usually an unconscious one and may indicate respect, insolence, humor, distance, or intimacy.

Norms

Norms of interaction and interpretation in a speech act include taking turns in speaking (if appropriate in the speaker's culture), knowing the proper voice level to express anger, and sharing understandings about such things as what to take seriously and what to discount. It includes knowing polite greeting forms and other "linguistic manners," like what not to talk about at the dinner table.

Genres

Some speech acts may be categorized in formal structures: poem, myth, tale, proverb, riddle, curse, prayer, oration, lecture, editorial. Even children are often expected to know a few of the forms appropriate to their culture, including the "Once upon a time . . ." of middle class English.

A change in any of these speech components may signal that some different linguistic rules should be in operation, but these are not the kind of rules found in grammar books. How they are acquired is an important but neglected consideration in our study of child language learning and total socialization.

CODE-SWITCHING

Naïve references are sometimes made to the "mixed-up" or "hybrid" language of bilinguals, as the so-called Tex Mex or Spanglish spoken in the southwestern United States or Puerto Rico. In fact, different languages (or different combinations of languages) are relevant and appropriate in different contexts. Poems are being written and formal speeches made in a mixture of Spanish and English, and the ability to switch codes effectively is recognized in many bilingual communities as an ability to be admired and cultivated. The switching itself communicates subtle meanings, and perhaps most importantly, identifies the speaker as a member of the bilingual rather than the monolingual community.

No speaker of any language is limited to a single linguistic code, although monolinguals are limited to switching varieties or registers within a single language. One of the communication skills which children learning a second language need to acquire is the ability to switch languages or varieties at will, and in accordance with the appropriate contexts, as discussed in the preceding section.

Children growing up in essentially segregated bilingual communities may acquire only its bilingual code and not encounter models or social support for the "standard" or monolingual form of either English or their ancestral language. It is crucial to recognize that their language is as logical and systematic as any other, and that it is more appropriate for communication in their home and neighborhood than the "foreign" languages of schools in Mexico or the United States. These "foreign" languages of the schools must be learned if children are to function effectively in that context, too, but this should be viewed as addition to (not replacement of) the language of their home.

Bilingual teachers who reject a child's language, insisting from the beginning on "standard" Spanish, French, or whatever they speak instead, are just as damaging to that child's self-concept and learning potential as those who feel he is without any valid language if he doesn't speak English.

Code-switching phenomena in bilingual communities can perhaps be best understood as responses to the different social relations that language signals. The ancestral language is almost always used with young children if there are grandparents in the home, but one or both parents may use mainly English, or switch from one to the other. Such switching is likely to be common between parents and bilingual friends in any case, since it signals closeness and informality. So-called standard monolingual forms of both languages are generally common only to more formal relations, and thus are seldom observed by young children at home.

Some bilinguals in the United States avoid speaking any language but English to their children in order to facilitate their assimilation into the mainstream Anglo culture. The fact that these children can then seldom participate fully in the bicultural community underscores the important functions of language, and the importance of cultivating bilingualism and code-switching skills—if our goal is a multicultural society.

FOR ADDITIONAL READING

BRENGELMAN, FRED, *The English Language: An Introduction for Teachers* (Englewood Cliffs, N.J.: Prentice-Hall, Inc., 1970).

BROWN, ROGER, *Words and Things: An Introduction to Language* (New York: The Free Press, 1958).

CAZDEN, COURTNEY B., VERA P. JOHN, and DELL HYMES, eds., *Functions of Language in the Classroom* (New York: Teachers College Press, Columbia University, 1972).

CICOUREL, AARON V., and others, *Language Use and School Performance* (New York: Academic Press, 1974).

FASOLD, RALPH and WALT WOLFRAM, *The Study of Social Dialects in American English* (Englewood Cliffs, N.J.: Prentice-Hall, Inc., 1974).

GUMPERZ, JOHN J. and DELL HYMES, eds., *Directions in Sociolinguistics: The Ethnography of Communication* (New York: Holt, Rinehart and Winston, 1972).

HERNANDEZ-CHAVEZ, EDUARDO, ANDREW D. COHEN, and ANTHONY F. BELTRAMO, eds., *El Lenguaje de los Chicanos: Regional and Social Characteristics of Language Used by Mexican Americans* (Arlington, Va.: Center for Applied Linguistics, 1975).

HYMES, DELL H., ed., *Language in Culture and Society: A Reader in Linguistics and Anthropology* (New York: Harper and Row, 1964).

LADO, ROBERT, *Linguistics Across Cultures* (Ann Arbor: University of Michigan Press, 1957).

LANGACKER, RONALD W., *Language and Its Structure: Some Fundamental Linguistic Concepts.* 2nd ed. (New York: Harcourt Brace Jovanovich, 1973).

TRUDGILL, PETER, *Sociolinguistics: An Introduction* (Middlesex, England: Penguin Books, 1974).

WOLFRAM, WALT, *Sociolinguistic Aspects of Assimilation: Puerto Rican English in New York City* (Arlington, Va.: Center for Applied Linguistics, 1974).

Cultural Foundations

CHAPTER 4

CULTURE, LANGUAGE, AND EDUCATION

The culture of a group of people includes all of the systems, techniques, and tools which make up their way of life. Many manifestations of culture can be readily seen: high-rise apartment buildings, brush shelters, cars, canoes, clothes, guns, bows and arrows. These are the physical artifacts of material culture. Manifestations of nonmaterial culture are much harder to observe, but equally important for understanding a people's way of life: custom, belief, values, means for regulating interaction with other humans and with the supernatural.

Because knowledge, perception, and behavior are so strongly influenced by culture, members of different cultural groups can never live in exactly the same "real" world. Nor can "basic" concepts ever be assumed to have exact correspondences across cultural boundaries. It is unlikely that the concepts labeled in English as *snow, blue, family,* or *good* can ever be equated exactly with categories in other cultures.

Language is a key component of culture. It is the primary medium for transmitting much of culture, making the process of language learning in children in part a process of enculturation. Children learning their native language are learning their own culture; learning a second language also involves learning a second culture to varying degrees, which may have very profound psychological and social consequences for both children and adults.

The vocabulary of a language provides us with an interesting re-flection of the culture of the people who speak it, an index to the way they categorize experience. The category labeled *snow* in English, for instance, is divided into seven different categories with seven different verbal labels for speakers of Eskimo, both reflecting and requiring a much more detailed perception of its variant characteristics than most English-speakers would ever have. An English-speaker to whom snow is very important, such as a ski enthusiast or a meteorologist, will be able to modify *snow* to indicate variant characteristics when this is required—*wet snow, packed snow, powder snow*—but such distinctions aren't re-quired by the language as they are in Eskimo. The Marshallese Islanders have little or no need to refer to snow, so their language does not reflect such perceptions, but they have sixty terms for parts of the coconut and coconut tree.

Many examples could be cited of the way language reflects a world view. Greek and some dialects of Quechua (an Indian language spoken in Peru and Bolivia) consider the future 'behind' you and the past 'ahead', instead of the future being 'ahead' as it is in English. According to Eugene Nida,[1] the Quechuas defend their logic by pointing out that we can 'see' the past, but not the future. Since we 'see' the past, it must be in front of our eyes, and the future that we cannot 'see' is behind. Color categories form another example. There is certainly no logical necessity for the way English-speakers divide the color spectrum, since it is obviously a continuum, and speakers of many other languages make the arbitrary points of division at quite different places along the scale (as suggested by the Navajo and Muskogean examples in Chapter 3). The meaning of any word is arbitrary and depends on the agreement of a group of speakers as to its symbolic value.

An interesting question is asked about this relationship between language and the other aspects of culture: to what extent is a language reflecting a world view, as cited above, or to what extent is a language shaping and controlling the thinking of its speakers by the perceptual requirements it makes of them?[2] Does a language which requires social distinctions to be made in order to choose the proper pronominal form (as Spanish and German do for the selection of *tu* versus *Vd.* or *Du* versus *Sie*) force speakers to think in terms of social "superiority" or

[1]Eugene A. Nida, "Principles of Translation as Exemplified by Bible Translat-ing," in *Language Structure and Translation: Essays by Eugene A. Nida* (Stanford, Calif.: Stanford University Press, 1975), p. 25.

[2]This is called the "Sapir-Whorf Hypothesis"; much has been written about it, including *Language, Thought, and Reality: Selected Writings of Benjamin Lee Whorf*, ed. John B. Carroll (Cambridge, Mass.: The M.I.T. Press, 1956).

"inferiority"? The answer to this question remains open to speculation, but we can feel quite sure that both sides contain elements of truth, that there is a correlation between the form and content of a language and the beliefs, values, and needs present in the culture of its speakers.

A great deal of cross-cultural misunderstanding occurs when the "meanings" of words in two languages are assumed to be the same, but actually reflect differing cultural patterns. Some are humorous, as when a Turkish visitor to the United States refused to eat a *hot dog* because it was against his beliefs to eat dog meat, or when some students from the Dominican Republic precipitated an argument on a Texas college campus by referring to the Texas students as *Yankees*. Some are much more serious, as when American Indian parents gave up their children for *adoption,* expecting them to return to their families at the end of the school year, and when a French couple on a trip to China took their pet poodle into a restaurant and requested some *dog food*. The dog was cooked and returned to their table on a platter.

Still more instances are never recognized as linguistic misunderstandings at all, but merely add to negative stereotypes of other cultural groups. Spanish-speakers unknowingly encounter negative attitudes from English-speakers for their use of the common expletive *Dios mío,* since the English translation 'My God' is much stronger than the Spanish, and socially disapproved of. The common use of the name *Jesús* in Spanish is regarded as bordering on the blasphemous by some English-speakers, who consider it taboo (and usually change it to *Jesse* at school).

It would be completely impossible to separate language from culture, even if it were desirable to do so, because of the solid embedding of cultural information in language use and interpretation. When English-speakers say *He's a truck driver,* we understand he drives trucks for a living, while few would give the same interpretation to *He's a Volkswagen driver.* The embedded cultural information is that people do not normally drive Volkswagens for a living as they do trucks, but can only own one to drive to and from another occupation.

Cultural information is also necessary to interpret *Mary is a telephone lineman, but she's a woman at heart* and to explain why **Mary is a secretary, but she's a woman at heart* is not a probable sentence in English. The culture-specific information required to understand these examples is that women in this culture are not normally telephone linemen, but they are frequently secretaries.[3]

In many cases the information required is shared by other cultures

---

[3]These examples were given by John Lawlor in a presentation at The University of Texas in 1972.

which have developed from Judeo-Christian or Graeco-Roman traditions, such as allusions to *the patience of Job* or a headline during a presidential campaign, "Wounded Knee is McGovern's Achilles Heel." Even reading a sports page ("The Dolphins Win the Super Bowl") demands a great deal of cultural information often not available to students of English as a second language, and not usually taken into account in ESL curricula.

The American educational system itself is a cultural invention. It is one which serves primarily to prepare middle class children to participate in their own culture. Most teachers are trained to meet the educational needs of only this group of children. Children from other cultures, including the lower class, are usually perceived as disadvantaged or deficient to the degree their cultural experiences differ from the mainstream, middle class "norms." (Our programs in compensatory education have been based largely on this rationale, to provide the middle class cultural experiences to children who have been "deprived" of them.)

We cannot fault our educational system for attempting to transmit the dominant American culture to all its students, since such enculturation is the essential purpose of education in all cultures. We *can* fault lack of provision or respect for children's culturally diverse backgrounds, however. We can ask our educational system to make aspects of the dominant culture a meaningful part of the children's experience without displacing or conflicting with the corresponding parts of their native cultures.

Teachers working with children from other groups must learn to see themselves and the school from a perspective of cultural relativity. They must learn to respect and be able to deal with the culturally different backgrounds which children bring to school. Every teacher of English as a second language is in the position of teaching a second culture as well, and every one should be able to fill the role of a cross-cultural interpreter in addition to serving as a second language instructor.

CULTURAL INFLUENCES ON LEARNING AND TEACHING

It has long been argued, often on the basis of relatively little evidence, that language difference as such, and a lack of knowledge of English in particular, constitutes a causative factor in the low scholastic achievement of students from non-English-speaking backgrounds. The argument seems to be a very plausible one in those cases where a child must learn entirely through the medium of English. Certainly he is at a disadvantage trying to comprehend and express himself in a foreign language, especially when other students with whom he must compete have already mastered English (a conclusion affirmed by the United States Supreme Court in its decision on Lau vs. Nichols). We must look further than the language differences to find a cause for this low scholastic achievement and inequitable opportunities, however, since we suspect that competence in English at school entry does not correlate as highly with academic success as do socioeconomic status and ethnic group membership.[4]

It seems clear from the information that we have about non-English-speaking students that economic deprivation and the social conditions associated with it do tend to interfere with second language learning and other aspects of school achievement. Present rather than future orientation, low educational levels of parents, and lack of books in the home, while cultural factors which may indeed inhibit school success, are related to social class rather than to ethnic or linguistic group membership. Poor English-speaking Blacks and Anglos have these same environmental "handicaps" when they enter school because they, too, are different from the mainstream middle class culture for which our educational system is geared. Even such apparently ethnic differences as family structure, child-rearing practices, and cooperative versus competitive coping behavior are largely dependent on socioeconomic status.[5]

Even more clearly affecting learning are the attitudes and motivation of children and their parents, many of which are culture-specific. Cultural attitudes and values most assuredly affect teaching as well, since educators acquire these as members of their own cultural group, learn and generally adopt those of the dominant group where it is different, and have different attitudes and expectations toward students from different minority cultures.

Man is a cultural animal; we are all in one way or another products of our culture, and much of our behavior, values, and goals are cul-

----

[4]Very interesting data supporting this hypothesis was collected by Betty Mace-Matluck in research for her thesis, "A Linguistic Profile of Children Entering Seattle Public Schools Kindergartens in September, 1971, and Implications for Their Instruction," (unpublished master's thesis, The University of Texas at Austin, 1972).

[5]Millard C. Madsen and A. Shapira, "Cooperative and Competitive Behavior of Urban Afro-American, Anglo-American, Mexican-American and Mexican Village Children," *Developmental Psychology*, 3, no. 1 (1970), 16–20; S. A. Wasserman, "Values of Mexican-American, Negro, and Anglo Blue-Collar and White-Collar Children," *Child Development*, 42 (1971) 1624–28; Spencer Kagan and Millard C. Madsen, "Rivalry in Anglo-American and Mexican Children of Two Ages," *Journal of Personality and Social Psychology*, 24 (1972) 214–20; and Philip E. Del Campo, "An Analysis of Selected Features in the Acculturation Process of the Mexican-American Elementary School Child" (unpublished doctoral dissertation, International University, San Diego, Calif., 1970).

turally determined. It is important to be aware of this, in order to understand both ourselves and those we teach. While we can never hope to be completely free of the biases of our own culture in teaching and evaluating our students (including interpreting test results), we can at least attempt to be fair and just—by perceiving our own biases and learning to recognize that cultural differences do not represent deficiencies.

THE NATURE OF STEREOTYPING

We have shown that some of the characteristics often ascribed to students of different ethnic groups are in fact stereotypes assigned by the dominant society, but we need to understand better how stereotypes operate and what the process of stereotyping entails.[6]

Social typing or categorization is a necessary part of our procedures for coping with the outside world. It allows us to quickly define our orientation to other individuals, and is a basis for our cultural sense of manners and other conventions of interpersonal relations. It is a means for establishing preliminary relationships.

As teachers, we would probably prefer to think that we always relate to all students (and their parents) as individuals, but it is easy to see why this cannot be true. In the first place, we must relate to the group of students in our class from the first day of school, and there is rarely an opportunity in advance to know each one well, unless we teach in the neighborhood where we live. The initial relationship with members of the class is guided by our expectations of what students that age are like, which we may have from prior experience or from our training, by our perception of ourselves, and by our attitudes toward the appropriate role for us to assume in that context, all of which are culturally conditioned. (The students also come to the encounter with a variety of expectations regarding the school and the appropriate behavior of adults as well as of themselves.) Based on these expectations and attitudes, a teacher may relate initially to a class with a set of behaviors ranging from benevolent grandmother to friend to drill sergeant. Even if we think we are just being ourselves, that is still dependent on our perceptions of self, the students, and the appropriate relationship between us in the school setting.

[6]For an excellent discussion of this process, see Roger D. Abrahams, "Stereotyping and Beyond," in *Language and Cultural Diversity in American Education,* ed. R. D. Abrahams and R. C. Troike (Englewood Cliffs, N.J.: Prentice-Hall, Inc., 1972) pp. 19–29.

Social typing of a group can indeed quickly be modified by the individual differences and needs we perceive, and a sensitive teacher is soon relating much of the time to specific students in all their diversity.

Initial social typing also controls our early relationships with our students' parents, other teachers (if we are new to the staff), the principal, nurse, janitor, cook. If we did not know how to relate appropriately to different groups of people before we were acquainted with them personally, we would be socially ineffective to say the least, and perhaps even unable to function normally in a society.

Social typing should thereby be seen as a positive and inevitable process. The typing may assume negative aspects, however, and then it ceases to be just a mode of socialization. It may become a means of disaffiliation or rejection, of rationalizing prejudice—the process of stereotyping.

Stereotyping is used to establish social distance and social boundaries, and a dominant group may impose stereotypes on another group to maintain and rationalize its subordination. It is often a process of defining a group in terms of what it does *not* do, and always involves prejudging as well as describing. From another perspective, stereotypes are often the negative side of in-group values. What the in-group values positively, the group being stereotyped is said to lack. This explains why, in spite of the fact that stereotypes are often applied to specific ethnic groups, they always have a great deal in common, as shown in the following paragraphs.

1. The in-group values cleanliness. A common stereotype is therefore that others are dirty, greasy, smelly. Middle class whites may objectively note that the lower socioeconomic classes frequently lack proper bathing facilities or changes of clothing, but may be surprised to discover a common stereotype Blacks hold of whites is that they "smell like dogs coming in out of the rain." Asians have a similar stereotype of Caucasians.

2. The in-group values human nature over animal nature. Their stereotypes therefore often express animal characteristics: "they eat like pigs," "they breed like rabbits." These may sound more positive, like "they're good athletes," or "they have great rhythm," and still be expressing the predominance in "them" of animal (physical) characteristics over the human (intellectual). The "pugnaciousness" of the Irish, "machismo" of the Latin Americans, and the "wine, women, and song" image of the Italians are also ascribed to this category.

3. The mainstream middle class group in this society values time as a commodity. They "spend" it, "save" it, even "buy" it; they "never put off to tomorrow what we can do today," they say that "a stitch in

time saves nine," and so forth. They place great emphasis on speed in learning, and consider time a critical factor in standardized tests. They stereotype others as operating on "Mexican time" or "Indian time," although recognizing the appropriateness of their own deviations from promptness, and there are endless jokes (by men) about women never being ready. Students must be on time for college classes, although a professor is allowed a degree of latitude commensurate with rank; patients must be on time for appointments, but doctors and dentists are never expected to be (patients may be suspicious of one who is and wonder why he doesn't have more business); guests who are on time for a cocktail party are likely to find the host and hostess not yet ready to receive them (more important guests, and especially a guest of honor should be later still). While the dominant society stereotypes other groups as "not thinking time is important," a return stereotype is that Anglos are mechanically run by clocks and value time over human relationships. No group takes into account the relativity of time when stereotyping another.

4. The in-group values change, and therefore stereotypes others as passive. This same dimension is evident when another group is seen as quaint, and when a member of the in-group says that a member of another group has "a negative self-image," when that other person is feeling a lack of control over environmental forces.

5. The in-group values independence and self-reliance, and stereotypes others as shy, backwards, or childlike. Teachers may perceive students as dishonest if they are too cooperative (especially in completing assignments and taking tests), and adults from the group being stereotyped may be perceived as lazy or lacking ambition.

It is important to identify stereotypes where they occur in our own thinking or in the educational establishment to which we belong. They are not always as transparent as they may seem when explicitly pointed out, but can usually be recognized by their negative statement of middle class values. With only enough of the wording changed to disguise the actual sources, the following list illustrates the kinds of stereotypes which can be found in lists of the characteristics of "disadvantaged" or other "culturally different" children in our professional literature:

> Their parents are less likely to belong to or attend church.   (This means: We value church-going.)
>
> They do not share the principle of cleanliness. "Water costs money or effort if it must be carried from an outdoor pump." (We value both cleanliness and industry.)

They do not understand the principles of saving. (We value thrift.)

They cannot put reason before emotion. (We value reason.)

They are freer and more social in their expressions of sex. (We value sexual restraint and self-control.)

They have not learned that doing one's duty and living up to the expectations of others pays off. (We value a "sense of responsibility.")

They believe the future is nonexistent. (We are "future-oriented"; cf. "The Grasshopper and the Ant.")

They believe education is an obstacle course to be surmounted until they can go to work. (We value formal education.)

Stereotyping, as well as social typing, may be an inevitable process, but it is an educational problem which can consciously be brought under control if the stereotypes are recognized. If not, they have two major repercussions in the classroom: they build a social barrier which inhibits communication and learning, and they affect the self-image of those who are typed.

There are indeed real differences between groups of people, and the answer lies in the recognition, understanding, and respect given to these real cultural differences, not in the proclamation that all people "are the same beneath the skin." This seemingly egalitarian assertion often hides an even deeper ethnocentric assumption, that all people are "like me."

ATTITUDES TOWARD LANGUAGE

One area of cultural differences within which stereotypes may develop is in attitudes toward language and its functions, and this is especially relevant to teachers of a second language.

Besides sharing common features of vocabulary, pronunciation, and grammar, each speech community shares a set of values regarding the uses of language in various contexts. These include judgments on the relative prestige of different regional and social varieties, on what is good and what bad language, on what features of speech are "defective," on linguistic criteria for group and role identifications, and on feelings about the appropriateness of different styles of language for self-expression on different occasions. There are also shared values regarding such things as the desirability of maintaining an ancestral language versus acquiring the national language, and the appropriateness of being bilingual.

Conflicting attitudes toward language create one of the greatest problems in cross-cultural communication between teachers and students (or their parents); misunderstandings often occur for this reason. When the differences are understood, they may be used as an educational base. When they are not, they create a formidable barrier to learning.

One cultural difference in language use which has already been mentioned is the difference in voice level normally used by some Native American groups and whites, with Native Americans interpreting the whites' level as anger and hostility and the whites interpreting the Native Americans' level as shyness or unfriendliness.

A child who looks directly at the teacher when talking or listening is considered honest, direct, straightforward by most Anglos and as disrespectful by most Mexican-Americans, Blacks, and Native Americans. The child who averts his eyes would be considered respectful by the latter and shifty or dishonest by many Anglos.

The standard middle class English speech patterns presented as a model in school are likely to be considered effeminate and thus rejected by lower class boys approaching adolescence, especially as these patterns are used by female teachers. The English of male aides and teachers or of older boys would be much more likely to be adopted by boys wanting to establish a male identity.

Social conventions differ. Each of these greetings is appropriate in some language: *How are you? Where are you from? How much money do you earn? What do you know? What is your name?*[7] In some cultures, it is inappropriate to speak at all when meeting someone.

There are also culture-specific ways to suggest that a visitor leave: some women say they have something to do, some that dinner is burning on the stove, some that they are expecting a delivery, and in some cultures that their husbands will beat them; some men glance at their watch, while in other cultures they may stand; children in our culture may say, "I think I hear your mother calling you." In some cultures there is no way at all to politely suggest that a guest should leave, and no one does so. Our own practices would be considered very rude in these contexts.

Cultural notions also differ on who should talk and when. The school supports the convention of talking one at a time (after raising one's hand and being called on) and not interrupting; other cultures would consider that rude, a sure sign that no one was interested in what the primary speaker was saying. Some cultures feel it is inappropriate

---

[7]David Abercrombie, "The Social Basis of Language," *English Language Teaching*, 3 (1948), 1–11.

for children to talk in the presence of adults, and others that it is inappropriate for women to talk in the presence of men.

Mitigation techniques also differ, and students encounter many problems in our schools when they come from cultures that do not use the same ones. A mainstream middle class child learns to avoid unpleasant assignments with such indirect excuses as *I'm tired. Can't I do that later?, Can I finish this first?,* or by nonverbal dawdling or daydreaming until the time is up. While often unsuccessful, the attempt brings no serious reproof. A student who has not learned these cultural patterns and says *No, I won't,* or just *No* (essentially meaning the same thing) will be considered belligerent and often threatened with the principal's office.

This same student may misunderstand the teacher who says *Wouldn't you like to do your arithmetic now?* and think she is really asking him a question.

Conflicting attitudes toward language usually operate at an inconspicuous level, but they may cause very obvious hostility or withdrawal. One second grader had solidly refused to say a word of English in class, although he followed the directions given in English by his teacher when they did not require a verbal response. When he was asked (in Spanish) why he didn't want to speak English, he almost shouted, *Porque soy Mexicano* 'Because I'm Mexican'. More common are the "shy" children who try not to be noticed, and the adults who contact them in school are often not really sure if they speak English or not. Both the hostile boy and the very shy are examples of students who are threatened by English.

No complete inventory exists of different social rules for language usage or of different attitudes toward language, but we must still consider both important components of teaching English as a second language. Breaking rules of grammar in English may make it difficult for students to be understood on some occasions, but breaking social rules of usage is much more serious; it will create ill will toward the speaker if the cultural differences are not understood. The teacher needs to be sensitive to areas where there may be differences in language use, and should make the initial assumption that a non-native speaker of English breaks a social rule because he doesn't know the rule, not because he is rude or insubordinate.

Sensitivity to the feelings of parents and students in a non-English-speaking community about such attitudes as the value they place on the maintenance of their native language and the acquisition of English is vital if the home and school are to be mutually supportive and not conflicting cultural forces in students' development.

LEARNING-STYLES AND FORMS OF EDUCATION

A second major area of cultural differences within which stereotypes may develop is in learning-styles and forms of education. Although our educational system most closely represents the culture of our mainstream middle class population, it has developed some attitudes, values, and expectations in its own right which set it apart as a subculture within our society in these respects. Successful advancement in the system quite naturally requires adoption of or adaptation to these concepts. Educators must be seen from this perspective as successfully acculturated (since they must have adapted themselves to the subculture in order to complete the years of training for certification); they are transmitters of these attitudes, values, and expectations to the next generation so that it, too, may "achieve" in school.

Educators must therefore learn about their own system of learning and realize that education does not have the same ends and means for members of different social groups. Stereotypes result if we assume that other systems of education are less advanced, or that students who don't succeed in our particular system are deficient in some respect. Since children learn how to learn from their families in early childhood, cultural differences are very well established by kindergarten or first grade.

A major difference involves notions of the purpose of education, although the requirement that it inculcate values in students which will support society seems to be generally valid. The cultural variation is present in what those values are, to what extent education should preserve the past, and to what extent it should encourage change. Our own culture equates progress with change and places a high priority on training students who may "better" society. While we teach history, the goal of that instruction is often that we not repeat the mistakes of the past or that we learn what has gone before so that it may provide a base for the new we wish to build. We also value individual independence and achievement, and we encourage our students to excel.

Others feel that the primary purpose of education is to preserve what is and has been, to learn the wisdom of the past, and to maintain harmony with God and nature. They may train students to value the common welfare over individual achievement, and to encourage service to society (the state). For instance, a traditional Turkish education consisted primarily of learning the Koran, the Chinese placed a priority on learning the wisdom of the ancient philosophers, and children being educated in the kibbutzes of Israel are indeed learning to value the common welfare over their own.[8] Major political or philosophical shifts in a country require shifts in education, as well, as evidenced by the recent revolution in the Chinese schools.

Another cultural difference involves who or what are considered the primary agents for education. We believe this responsibility is vested in a special formal institution we call the school, which is often set apart from the community it serves. Others feel that parents have the major responsibility for teaching their own children, or that only the elders in a community should teach the young what they have learned. Still others place the heaviest responsibility for the education of young children on their older brothers or sisters, or their uncles and aunts.

To some extent, the identity of the chief educational agent determines which mode of instruction is most widely used. Our schools emphasize a *technical* mode in which teaching and learning are fully conscious processes, there is explicit instruction from teacher to student, and reasons are often given as mistakes are corrected. Elders usually teach by admonition, and also correct what they consider mistakes of the young (but less often provide reasons for the correction); instruction often has a binary yes–no character. To some degree an *informal* mode of education operates in all cultures, usually at an unconscious level and involving learning by imitation of models, but this degree varies greatly among different social groups. The technical mode which we emphasize may be inevitable whenever large groups of children are taught at the same time.

Children in different cultures also learn to learn in different ways. Our schools stress learning by doing, and trial-and-error learning—"if at first you don't succeed, try, try again." Language plays a completely pervasive role in our educational system for teaching, learning, and evaluation with verbal explanations, questions, and answers essential to the process. We consider time an important element, emphasize speed in learning, and encourage students to guess if they don't know.

These procedures are an extension of the predominant child-rearing patterns in our culture, and middle class children thus experience a relatively smooth transition between learning at home and learning at school. At home parents provide objects for them to manipulate, encourage exploration, and laugh when they try and fail, entreating them to try again. We reward children for *doing* things. We interact verbally with them a great deal, and we ask and encourage questions as a part of our teaching. Time is important from the beginning. There is a time for bottles, a time for baths, and a time for naps. Later we have meal

---

[8]Melford E. Spiro, "Education in a Communal Village in Israel," *The American Journal of Orthopsychiatry*, 25 (1955), 283–92.

time, story time, and a time to watch cartoons on television. We expect and often demand rigid age-graded behavior, worrying if the first step or the first word doesn't appear on time, and scolding for "acting like a baby" when that stage is passed.

Education in many other cultures stresses learning by memory and rote, or by observation (without doing, and without explanation). Many social groups consider it highly inappropriate for anyone to try to do something he has not already learned how to do correctly by observation. To try and fail would be humiliating. It may be considered impolite for children to ask adults questions, or this too may be considered an inappropriate mode of learning. In some of these cases children's questions are discouraged by adults conveying the concept that children should observe and think so they will know the answer for themselves. Time may be irrelevant to learning; many cultures value correctness more than speed.

These different styles of learning are also very natural extensions of infant-rearing practices. Infants are often physically confined by being wrapped up in some way and carried with the mother, another adult, or older child wherever they go. Allowing a young child to explore his environment other than by visual and auditory observation may be considered not only inappropriate but highly dangerous, an abdication of adult responsibility. Most cultures do not have our compulsion for rigid schedules, and children may eat when they are hungry, sleep when they are tired, and accompany the family on all occasions without concern for a specific bedtime. While all social groups expect and require prescribed behavior of their adults (*adult* usually being defined as postpubescent), many allow children great freedom, not demanding rigid age-graded behavior.

It is obvious that children who learn to learn in one culture and then must learn in the modes of another must experience some confusion and dislocation in the process. They are unfamiliar with the school structure, the expectations of the teacher, and the classroom procedure. They may encounter very different values which are being considered essential for learning (for example, cleanliness, attendance, and punctuality). They may find values which they have been taught are penalized or rejected (not asking questions, not attempting to do what you are not sure of being able to do successfully, being very concerned for correctness even on a timed test).

Having made the case for language and education being inseparable from culture, we are really saying that teaching English as a second language entails teaching elements of English as a second culture, as well. We should give thought to minimizing interference in the learning process, and consider the cultural content an *addition* of new concepts and behaviors to be used when appropriate (in school), and not a *replacement* of home culture, just as we should consider the English language itself an addition rather than a replacement for the home language.

Once we recognize and understand the cultural differences in learning-styles among our own students, we have a choice to make. We may choose to adapt our educational system to the learning-styles of the students, or we may choose to have children adapt their learning-styles to the expectations and requirements of our educational system.

Most educators will choose the latter alternative in practice, while admitting that the former would ideally be best. While changing the system is a desirable long-range goal, children entering school now will indeed be seriously handicapped in achievement if they do not learn how to operate within it.

Some degree of adaptation of children to the school culture is a reasonable expectation, but it is at least equally reasonable to expect some adaptation in reverse. Even without major institutional changes, classroom teachers can help students develop bicultural competence by being understanding, accepting of differences, and flexible enough in organization and instruction to allow for different styles of learning.

ROLE IDENTIFICATION AND GROUP MEMBERSHIP

In addition to learning how to learn, the early socialization of children involves learning a role. Initial role acquisition includes learning what is appropriate and expected behavior when relating to different members within the family, and then to different classes of individuals within the wider social group. As with modes of learning, most children find the new roles they assume when beginning school a rather natural extension of their earlier socialization experiences. For some, previously learned patterns of social interaction are not of value to the school situation, and they must acquire all new roles.

These behavioral variations add to the variable features of language, dress, skin hue, and economic level and form the complex unit perceived by the school as the culturally different student.

It is uncomfortable to be considered different in this categorical sense, even as we recognize that both individual and group differences are inevitable. More than that, we even recognize that "variety is the spice of life," and yet the desire to be alike is precisely the basis of peer-group pressure.

Most of our discomfort in referring to or being identified as members of social groups is because of the stereotyping so frequently associated with such identification, and the pejorative connotations labels for groups may engender. Members of the dominant group think nothing of viewing oppressed minorities stereotypically—all Blacks look alike, all Spanish surnames are to be retained, and so forth, but find it offensive if they themselves are not seen as individuals, but are rejected or threatened because they are white or middle class. So long as the categorization is at a distance, and not threatening, it may be viewed as merely quaintly amusing, and the information about it may have no effect in helping toward understanding. To be a member of a minority group, and to be viewed stereotypically, and to know that you are being so viewed, must be objectionable except to one who has "accepted his place."

Both adults and children have diverse attitudes about their social classification, as perceived by them or by others. Most value their own group membership. Some reject their own group and wish to change. This is always a possibility in our society, using such means as education, marriage, or emigration (including just moving across town). Many may wish or need to function as members of more than one social group and be bicultural.

These attitudes can be viewed as positive forces, and all can be compatible with learning a second language and with other school achievement, but they are often viewed in a negative light. Those who value their own group membership and don't wish to acculturate to the dominant group are treated as not well adjusted to our society. Those who reject their own group and wish to change are viewed as traitors to family and old friends. Those who wish to belong to more than one social group may be mistrusted by both, and seen as spies.

Whatever choice is made regarding group membership, language is a key factor, an identification badge, for both self and outside perception. A famous example is Eliza Doolittle of *Pygmalion* and *My Fair Lady,* who with the aid of linguist Henry Higgins moved from the Cockney lower class of London to a social group that mingled with kings.

The importance of language in establishing role identification and group membership is recognized (often unconsciously) even by young children. When I was teaching kindergarten in California, I assigned Spanish-speaking and English-speaking children to alternate chairs around the tables in order to maximize the children's opportunity to use the English vocabulary and structures I was teaching. One boy started speaking English with a lisp, although he did not lisp in Spanish. The answer was his English-speaking friend, who had recently lost his front teeth. The Spanish speaker was obviously identifying with a peer model, and not with his teacher. I reassigned him to sit by a boy who didn't lisp and he soon acquired a normal pronunciation. But he continued to lisp when the deviant pronunciation was appropriate—whenever he talked to his lisping friend. The second grade boy I discussed earlier who refused to use English because *"soy Mexicano"* is another example of a child whose language is tied to group membership. In this case the child wished to retain a unique group identity and rejected English as he rejected identification with the school culture.

Diversity of language even within a single speech community, such as the American English-speaking community, provides a great deal of information about speakers' social identities. Speakers of English (like speakers of other languages) regularly use dialect variables as a basis for judging others' social background, prestige, and even personality characteristics. Such concepts as status and role are not permanent qualities of language itself, but abstract communication symbols which are always perceived in relation to a particular social context.

Language probably serves this function because it is the principal medium for mediating and manipulating social relationships in our society. It is carried out in terms of culturally standardized patterns which children acquire as they learn to communicate and as part of their socialization (or enculturation). It is used to symbolize one's role in society, one's relationship with particular listeners, and even sets of attitudes and values.

As children learn their language and their culture they learn, in effect, to be a Mexican American, Anglo, Navajo, Greek, etc., or more accurately, a member of a small subgroup of that larger social classification. While such self-classification has a positive identity function, mistakes which educators may make in classifying students can have grave consequences in education. They need to be corrected.

First, race has no correlation with culture. Race is determined by genetic traits, and culture by diffusional ones. People who are of the same race may belong to different cultures, and people who belong to the same culture may be of different races. Where a group has been socially isolated or has recently immigrated, there may be an identification of certain cultural traits with a particular ethnic group, but this is, historically speaking, accidental and transitory.

Second, surnames should never be used as a guide to students' linguistic competence. Many schools make the mistake of assuming that any student named Sanchez must speak Spanish, and assign him to ESL or bilingual classes accordingly. In some cases, unfortunately still too common, six-year-old children designated Spanish-surnamed are automatically assigned to pre-firsts on the assumption that they won't be able to succeed in first grade without an extra year of instruction. In one school, a Spanish-surnamed boy was retained while his half brother was promoted because the latter had an Anglo name. A surname usually indicates the ethnic origin of part of a student's ancestry, but it does not indicate language competence or present group membership.

Third, the so-called disadvantaged do not constitute a homogeneous group in any respect. The notions "poverty" and "disadvantaged" are culturally defined, and relative only to the dominant group that does the classification. Such group identity is not a perception from within unless the typing of the dominant group is adopted. When children escape this label and succeed, they are likely to say as adults, "I didn't really know we were poor." Some minority group college students are upset to find out for the first time in education classes that they are considered disadvantaged.

Finally, there are no culturally based categories of smartness or intelligence, except insofar as intelligence may in part be culturally defined. Testing biases may systematically discriminate against cultural groups that differ from the groups to which the test-makers or "normative" population belong.

Assigning students to social boxes on the basis of such misunderstandings and stereotypes can be very detrimental to their education, since the expectations they generate can easily become self-fulfilling prophesies for both teachers and students.

Recognizing the viability of other cultures and the importance of the languages of different cultural groups to their maintenance of their cultures, we may want to question the importance of teaching English as a second language at all to minority groups or immigrants in the United States, or perhaps even question the importance of teaching English anywhere in the world.

The answer is that it is very important indeed.

In the first place, English is the single national language of the United States. It is important for the unity of the nation for all its citizens to be able to use the same language, and essential for individuals if they are to enjoy any degree of social or economic mobility within the larger American society, participate in its democratic processes, have access to knowledge and information, and not be at a disadvantage when dealing with the power structure.

Furthermore, English is an international language, and used as a lingua franca in many parts of the world. When Arabs talk to Russians or Chinese with Peruvians, English is often the medium of communication. English is the official language for all international airline traffic, and it is interesting to realize that passengers' safety depends on the pilot's and controller's ability to understand and be understood in English. International economics is also a factor in the use of English, since it is probably the most widely used language for trade and tourism around the world.

English also has important uses in international education, in as much as textbooks in many technical and scientific fields are available only in English. It is not uncommon in a foreign university to have lectures and discussions conducted in the national language, but texts and other resource books in English, and much advanced schooling of foreign students still takes place in the United States or England. There are not enough university slots in many countries, or they may not yet have developed programs in all areas which are needed.

The reasons a student has for learning English will make a difference in what kind of English he needs, what degree of competence he needs to achieve, and to some extent what methods and instructional materials we will select. The TESL (second language) versus TEFL (foreign language) distinction is usually made on the basis of the situation in the country, that is, whether English is an official language or not, rather than on the student's purposes in learning or using it. The national situation therefore determines something about how the language is to be taught, and how it fits into the total educational picture (that is, as medium or as object).

For most learners of English, there is a primary need for shared vocabulary. The next degree of importance probably belongs to grammar, since syntax carries part of the meaning load in English. In particular those who will use English in learning and communicating in technical fields will need quite complex grammatical forms. Pronunciation is of least importance for most purposes, at least if the primary performance criterion is intelligibility.

But we have already established that there is a great deal more involved in language use than mere intelligibility, and criteria of group identity and related social attitudes must also be taken into account. Along these dimensions, pronunciation assumes a far more important role. It may be a major key to group identity because it is the most readily perceived variant in language use, but in any case pronunciation has often provided a focal point for social discrimination.

A person who wishes to reject his native culture and be accepted completely into an English-speaking one has no choice but to place a high priority on acquiring nearly-native English pronunciation. No matter how completely he adopts the values and behaviors of the dominant group, it will seldom fully accept him as long as he sounds "different." (Exceptions are made, of course, for the very wealthy, powerful, or well educated.)

A balanced bicultural individual, who identifies with and is accepted by both social groups, needs complete bilingual competence as well. He should ideally acquire complete communicative skills in both his native and adopted language, including a very high degree of control over both phonological systems.

Which of the three group identification categories a student is in is not a decision which the school can make, since it is a social and not an academic decision. The answer for any one teacher with a heterogeneous class is to be sensitive to the needs and attitudes of individuals as well as the group, to provide access to the full range of English skills for those who may need or want them, and not to discriminate against students who may resist total linguistic acculturation.

It is regrettable that our dominant society often demands such a traumatic choice between languages and cultures; many others do not. It is a reflex of an endemic intolerance, a kind of domestic neocolonialism, which hopefully can be changed.

VALUES, EXPECTATIONS, AND GOALS

We have already recognized that teachers and students may have different values, and that one of the functions of education is to transmit the attitudes and values that will enable students to "achieve" in school. Some of the differences in values which may create conflict in the classroom are the importance of cooperation versus competition, of aggression versus compliance, of anonymity versus self-assertion; the importance of time and of cleanliness.

This list should sound familiar, but it is an abstraction that may mean little in terms of classroom practices. Conflict of values is very real in education. Test-taking requires competition, for instance, and we consider cooperative behavior cheating in such contexts; asking questions or volunteering answers requires self-assertion, and we penalize students who value anonymity by not being sensitive to their unasserted needs and strengths.

A few years ago I was having difficulty keeping all the pieces for reading games in my classroom, and was obviously the victim of a six-year-old thief. When I finally saw him stuffing his pockets one day, I decided to recover the loot after school instead of in front of the class and to have a little talk with his mother at the same time. I valued the reading games very highly, as all teachers who have made their own material will understand, because their preparation was very time-consuming, I had spent my own money on them, and besides, they were nearly useless as instructional aids with pieces missing.

The mother of my "thief" did not speak English, so our verbal communication was very limited, but I did understand. I was not invited inside the house, but I could see that there was no furniture at all in the living room—and two preschoolers were sitting on the bare floor playing with my games! Their brother had valued *their* pleasure above learning to read or my time.

This story has a happy ending because I traded some of my own children's toys for the games, but I wonder how many times I have not understood the reasons for a student's actions. Too often we condemn behavior as a simple negation of a value we hold, rather than recognizing that an alternative value may be in operation.

Our educational goals are not limited to instructional objectives, but include the enculturation or socialization of students to our values and expectations as well. This involves a weighty responsibility and requires careful thought, because, for good or ill, we often succeed.

Teachers hold a tremendously prestigious and influential position in the eyes of children, and this carries with it a responsibility which we cannot take lightly. We often win out in a conflict where the student's family says or does one thing and the teacher says another. When teachers tell students what they should eat for breakfast, for instance, children may feel ashamed because their family doesn't do—or can't afford to do—the "right thing." When a student is kept home from school to care for an infant in the absence or illness of his mother, the teacher says this is "bad." The student is caught between value systems and between allegiance to home *or* school. He will have to stay home, but if the teacher is succeeding in his enculturation, he will feel very guilty about it.

Accepting the goal of success in school often requires alienation from home, family, friends, and cultural heritage, and this is a terrible price to ask children to pay.

Learning English as a second language should never make this requirement of students, but the alternative is to put some rather stringent requirements on ourselves.

We should understand the nature of language and the socially and psychologically identifying significance of language differences.

We should be able to communicate effectively with students, understanding the languages and cultures of both home and school.

We should recognize the differences between these systems and both the potential conflicts and the opportunities they may create for students.

We should understand the rate and sequence of linguistic development in the students' first and second languages, including 1) group and individual variations with the "normal" range, and 2) the interrelationships of language development with cognitive development and socialization, including regional and social variation in usage.

We should know methods and possess skills for adding the necessary features of school language and culture to the student's experience and understanding without damaging his concept of himself, his home, or his community.

We should implement the concept of accepting the student where he is and building on the strengths he brings to school, rather than rejecting him and trying to remake him in the school's image.

In all of this, we must keep our eye on the fact that in teaching English as a second language, we are not simply teaching an alternative set of labels for the same reality. In teaching a second language we are teaching culturally different patterns of perception, of communication, and of affect—in short, we are teaching a second culture.

We must learn to understand both the medium and the content of what we are teaching, and learn to be sensitive to the differences between what we are teaching and what the student brings to the classroom, so that our teaching becomes an aid and not a hindrance to the full realization of the student's potential as a human being.

FOR ADDITIONAL READING

BROWN, INA CORINNE, *Understanding Other Cultures* (Englewood Cliffs, N.J.: Prentice-Hall, Inc., 1963).

BURLING, ROBBINS, *Man's Many Voices: Language in Its Cultural Context* (New York: Holt, Rinehart and Winston, 1970).

BURMA, JOHN H., ed., *Mexican-Americans in the United States* (Cambridge, Mass.: Schenkman, 1970).

FITZPATRICK, JOSEPH, *Puerto Rican Americans: The Meaning of Migration to the Mainland* (Englewood Cliffs, N.J.: Prentice-Hall, Inc., 1971).

HALL, EDWARD T., *The Silent Language* (Garden City, N.Y.: Doubleday, 1959).

IANNI, FRANCIS A. and EDWARD STORY, *Cultural Relevance and Educa-*

tional Issues: Readings in Anthropology and Education (Boston: Little, Brown and Company, 1973).

KIMBALL, SOLON T., *Culture and the Educative Process: An Anthropological Perspective* (New York: Teachers College Press, Columbia University, 1974).

KLUCKHOHN, CLYDE, *Mirror for Man* (New York: McGraw-Hill, 1949).

MIDDLETON, JOHN, ed., *From Child to Adult: Studies in the Anthropology of Education* (Garden City, N.Y.: The Natural History Press, 1970).

MOORE, JOAN W., *Mexican Americans* (Englewood Cliffs, N.J.: Prentice-Hall, Inc., 1970).

Current Trends
in TESL

CHAPTER 5

The field of teaching English as a second language has entered a period of controversy and rapid change. Many of the ideas which have been accepted virtually as dogma in the past are now being rejected or held in question, and many new ideas on the nature of language, on learning, and on the goals of teaching are appearing, but there is still lacking a coherent new methodology to bring these ideas into practice, and to replace the old. Furthermore, many former TESL programs have become components of bilingual programs, but they have not yet developed integrated methods and content, nor in many cases even resolved the problem of how instruction in the students' first language should relate to instruction in English.

While such a state of transition places heavier burdens on those who might prefer to rely completely on ready-made lessons (whose adequacy must now be questioned), it is very healthy for teachers to be assessing—and changing—their practices in the light of their adequacy in meeting students' needs.

AN ASSESSMENT OF NEEDS AND PRACTICES

No matter what particular methods and curriculum models are expounded, or what the ethnic or linguistic diversity of the students taught, there is general agreement that these students' educational and psychological needs compose a common core, including:

68

Recognition and acceptance of students' previous linguistic, conceptual, and cultural experience as a base on which to build, rather than as a handicap to further learning

Respect for the values and traditions of their cultural heritage

Comfortable identity as individuals, and as members of a family, a community, and a nation

Positive expectations from self, family, and school

Continued and unbroken conceptual development

The extension of language skills (listening, speaking, reading, and writing) in functional contexts of learning and communication

Access to social, educational, and economic mobility

Success

The traditional educational program in American schools, which has been rigidly monocultural and monolingual in orientation, has failed in large measure to meet these needs for the thousands of students who come from different linguistic and cultural backgrounds. We should ask why, and whether specialized TESL programs have been doing better.

Recognition and acceptance of prior linguistic, conceptual, and cultural experiences as a base on which to build. Traditional methods and materials, including tests, are based on the premises that students in the system have acquired English in the natural way in their preschool years, that their conceptual development and socialization should have been following expected norms, and that differences in developmental patterns and experiences constitute deficiencies in need of remediation. Any linguistic experience other than in English and any cultural experience other than in mainstream America is treated as irrelevant for purposes of assessment or instruction, or worse, is depreciated, and teachers are not trained to recognize or capitalize on it. Nor has traditional TESL instruction generally recognized or built on previous linguistic development in another language, since it has generally either ignored or actively repressed it. And while bilingual education represents major progress in meeting this need, we can see Spanish instructional material used in the Southwest or New York which was prepared for students in Spain or in Mexico, or bilingual teachers criticizing their students' Spanish, or French, or Chinese in the mistaken belief that it is a corrupt and deficient form of the "true" language.

Respect for the values and traditions of students' cultural heritage. Educational goals are not limited to instructional objectives, but include the enculturation or socialization of students to group values and expectations a   ⁄ell. Values of the traditional school system are often in conflict with those of different cultures in terms of styles of learning, expected behavior in relation to peers and elders, and methods of coping with conflict. To the extent that the school has succeeded in enculturating students without regard for cultural differences, it has often destroyed respect for the values and traditions of their homes.

Traditional teacher-training programs and teacher-selection processes have not seemed even to recognize diverse cultural patterns, such as learning processes, value systems, and family roles and organization as important areas for study and preparation. Regrettably, teacher-training programs in TESL and in bilingual education are thus far doing little better. Cultural sensitivity and understanding is often assumed of someone born to the student's ethnic group and beyond the reach of anyone who is not. Yet we often observe minority-group teachers consciously teaching the behavior of the majority group, and we can see such teachers and administrators who have themselves rejected their own ethnic heritage reject students who have a cultural identity they do not wish to share. Common ethnic background can be helpful in providing role models and promoting empathy, but it does not automatically, without special training, assure an appreciation and acceptance of cultural differences.

We each have our cultural beliefs, values, and expectations. This ethnocentricity is inherent in our very nature as human beings. But teachers who intend to work with students from a different cultural and linguistic background need to bring this humanness to the surface, compare it with that of others, and recognize the differences which inescapably exist. Because culture operates at the very deepest level of consciousness, we are often unaware of its presence in ourselves, and fail to observe it in others, or to recognize the differences not as departures from our own norms and expectations, but as valid norms to be respected in their own right.

Comfortable identity as individuals, and as members of a family, a community, and a nation.   Language is a key factor in establishing role identification and group membership. Language serves this function because it is the principal medium for mediating and manipulating social relationships in a society. The function is carried out in terms of culturally standardized patterns which children acquire as they learn to communicate and as part of their socialization. These patterns are used to symbolize one's role in society, one's relationship with particular listeners, and even one's attitudes and values.

This is recognized, either implicitly or explicitly, by the educators who equate learning English with Americanization, for English is indeed our national language and essential for full participation in the larger society. But they have not recognized that development and maintenance of a student's first language may be critical for his identification with and membership in his family and community, or that his chances for full participation and membership in the dominant national society may be enhanced, rather than threatened, if he is secure in his ethnic and linguistic identity. An English-only policy in the schools has been educationally, socially, and psychologically damaging to students from non-English-speaking backgrounds.[1]

Positive expectations from self, family, and school.   One of the most questionable of educational practices from the standpoint of announcing (and then further generating) negative expectations is the homogeneous grouping of students by anticipated achievement levels, often in terms of their fluency in English. While "special" classes may be defended theoretically as providing for "special" needs, in practice the educational and affective stigma attached to them by students, parents, and teachers violates one of the students' most basic needs. Prolonged segregation for second language instruction on the basis of student characteristics is probably illegal, and is educationally unsound as well.[2] Research has clearly shown that language learning is most effective when it is motivated by the need for communication with peers who are native speakers.

Continued and unbroken conceptual development.   Learning begins in infancy, and early conceptual development normally coincides with first language acquisition, when the young child learns the words to label objects, attributes, and ideas, and the grammatical structures to express their relationships. Formal education builds on this early learning, with language itself gradually replacing direct experience as the

---

[1] Wallace E. Lambert, "Culture and Language as Factors in Learning and Education" (paper presented at the convention of Teachers of English to Speakers of Other Languages in Denver, Colo., March 1974).

[2] Thomas M. Hale and Eva C. Budar report that students attending "special" TESOL classes in Hawaii strongly resented that assignment, showed no greater competence in English than those who did not attend, and that "... those who spent two to three periods of the six-period school day in special TESOL classes were being more harmed than helped" ["Are TESOL Classes the Only Answer?," in *Focus on the Learner: Pragmatic Perspectives for the Language Teacher*, ed. John W. Oller, Jr. and Jack C. Richards (Rowley, Mass.: Newberry House, 1973), pp. 290–300]. This is also the general conclusion of the comprehensive report of the United States Commission on Civil Rights [*A Better Chance to Learn: Bilingual-Bicultural Education*, United States Commission on Civil Rights Clearinghouse Publication 51 (May 1975)].

primary medium for conceptual development. When students do not know the language of instruction, however, the traditional educational system has halted their conceptual development to await the learning of English. The resultant temporal retention or retardation of students has had a high positive correlation with their academic failure and drop-out rate.[3] The recognition of the need for students to continue their conceptual development while they are learning English has been a major impetus in the movement for bilingual education in this country.

The extension of language skills in functional contexts of learning and communication.   The traditional educational system has either ignored the existing language skills of non-English-speaking students or actively tried to repress them as barriers to English competence. Even when the native language has been maintained as the primary mode of communication in the home, church, and community, many thousands of our citizens have grown up illiterate in their first language and unable to use it adequately in other contexts.

Traditional TESL instruction has also failed to fulfill this need in the students' second language in those instances where it has taught words and structures in and of themselves. In segregated or "pull-out" classes, there has not been adequate consideration of the basic purpose of language for communication, nor of correlation with students' need to learn in content areas, nor of their need to learn to read.

Equal access to social, educational, and economic opportunity. English is the national language of the United States, as well as the world's leading international language, and is therefore the key to social, economic, and educational opportunity in our society. These are valid and compelling reasons for retaining English language and content instruction in all of our educational programs. But because little or no special provision has been made for students who enter school with limited competence in English, they have frequently failed to achieve social and economic status as adults equal to English speakers of the same ability and ambition, and they have generally completed a lower than average level of education, even after five or ten years of instruction in English. Some succeed admirably, of course, but often at great personal cost. There are surely no simple remedies, although partial answers undoubtedly include greater sensitivity of the school staff to cultural differences, greater relevance of language and content instruction to

---

[3]United States Commission on Civil Rights, *The Unfinished Education*, Report 2 of the Mexican American Educational Series (Washington, D.C.: U. S. Government Printing Office, October 1971).

student needs, better instructional materials and facilities, and improved pre- and in-service staff development. Social factors are also undoubtedly important, as are community attitudes and level of fiscal support.

Relative failure in these areas does not warrant the elimination of the traditional core curriculum; this would not serve students' common needs in the existing system. It does, however, warrant change.

Success.

It is an old but often true cliché that nothing succeeds like success; the converse, in which failure forms a vicious circle feeding upon itself, is also often bitterly true. Students from different cultural and linguistic backgrounds are penalized for their prior learnings rather than helped to new ones, and failure becomes a pattern of expectation for pupil and teacher alike, destroying motivation and alienating the student from the school and from learning. The failure of students to learn must be interpreted as the failure of the school to teach.

Do present TESL and bilingual programs increase student success? In quantitative terms, we frankly don't know. Good ones do; bad ones do not. Programs in and of themselves do not have the answer. The keys are teachers, methods, and content.

NEW DIRECTIONS

Multicultural education.

The first direction of change can be seen in teachers. The TESL profession within the United States has historically been assimilationist in its rationale for English instruction. It has been charged since its inception with teaching English overseas, or to foreign students who needed it to study in American universities, or to immigrants who needed it to find jobs or to become citizens and who generally wanted to become assimilated. With the realization that many thousands of students in our public schools are also learning English as a second language, the primary focus shifted to ESL classes at the elementary and secondary levels, still with the goal of assimilating these students as rapidly as possible into mainstream American language, culture, and education. The national professional organization (Teachers of English to Speakers of Other Languages, or TESOL), which now identifies members' diverging interests within the field, is showing another change in primary focus: a plurality of its membership is mainly concerned with bilingual education. This seems a sure sign that the profession is moving away from its assimilationist roots and toward an acceptance of the viability of multicultural education.

A related and necessary current trend in both theory and methodology is relating the use of language to its total cultural context. We may expect this to be an increasingly central focus in materials at all levels, particularly as progress is made in research on what anthropologists call the ethnography of speaking. Their techniques enable us to objectify information about all of the verbal and nonverbal routines, systems, and repertoires that are necessary for effective social communication.

Much less valid research is forthcoming in areas concerning, for example, the different learning styles and value systems of various cultures, so here for the present we must aim to be sensitive to possible areas of differences and conflicts rather than rely on specific information. We must for the time being, in fact, beware of those lists of cultural differences which have been published in the educational literature, but which are dangerously stereotypic in nature.

In terms of classroom methods and content, multicultural education must consist of more than just celebrating holidays or singing folksongs or eating particular foods; such an approach does not get beyond the surface of culture and in fact often distorts the impression of other cultures. Moreover, such an approach fails to create real understanding because it does nothing to affect the ethnocentric bias of the whole educational system.

Multicultural education involves the selection or development of culturally appropriate instructional material, with pre- and in-service staff development and sensitization, with student and program evaluation, and with classroom organization and procedures. Where successful, it will:

> Develop understanding and respect for cultural differences
>
> Adapt teaching styles, classroom organization and management to accommodate the styles of learning and values taught in the students' homes
>
> Adapt educational content for maximum relevance to the bilingual–multicultural community
>
> Increase understanding and respect for the values and traditions of each group's cultural heritage
>
> Enhance students' positive feelings of identity as individuals, and as members of a family, a group, a community, and a nation

These goals can be furthered in a wide variety of ways, including:

> Accepting and reinforcing behavior which is highly valued in the home, and not encouraging behavior which a student's family considers disrespectful and rude

Helping to resolve specific conflicts which may arise between the home and school cultures; for example, caring for a younger brother or sister versus regular school attendance

Including positive contributions of various cultures to studies of history, fine arts, inventions, discoveries, and current events

Selecting appropriate types of food for discussion in a health unit, and including relevant family or community structure in a social studies lesson

Providing for different styles of learning in instructional activities, including cooperative as well as competitive, and observational as well as participative

Prerequisite for the implementation of any such educational strategies are the sensitivity and awareness of staff to the nature of culture and its diversity. A mistaken egalitarianism should not be allowed to damage students by ignoring crucial differences.

Bilingual instruction.   One well-recognized development within the area of bilingual instruction is the establishment of bilingual education programs for major language groups, which by definition must include content instruction (such as science, social studies, or mathematics) in a language other than English. Beyond these, there is growing concern and urgent need for providing unbroken conceptual development as well for students whose native language is spoken by too few in a school district to make a full bilingual program feasible or in areas where a full bilingual program is not practicable or desirable for some other reason.

The change taking place is twofold: first, the recognition of the academic and social importance to students of "keeping up" with their English-speaking peers in the "normal" curriculum structure, and the recognition that translation support while acquiring English is not a barrier to learning. On the contrary, supplementary translation in their dominant language will profit students with limited competence in English in at least the following ways:

By insuring that the content of classes being conducted in English has meaning

By increasing the students' possibilities for success in English content classes

By increasing their attention and motivation by increasing their level of understanding and participation

These goals may be accomplished through a combination of educational strategies used in conjunction with English content instruction:

Informal and regular assistance from a content teacher who is bilingual in English and the students' native language and who can provide translation or explanation as necessary

Individual or small group tutorials with a bilingual teacher, aide, or advanced student

Telephone tutorials (A phone number is provided which students can call to ask questions in their native language about the content of their courses. A teacher, aide, or other staff member who speaks Greek or Arabic, for instance, might thus provide tutorial assistance during specified hours for a few students who are rather widely dispersed in the school system both by location and by grade level.)

Cassette recordings of instructional content either translated or summarized in each student's native language (For languages not spoken by any school staff member, these can be produced with the assistance of an adult bilingual in the student's family or community, or with a professor or foreign student at a nearby university.)

For students who are literate in their native language, supplementary books or translations and summaries of the English texts

The strategies suggested here are already being provided for many students in relatively homogeneous linguistic communities, but their applicability (and feasibility) where five or more languages are spoken in a single class has yet to be tried and tested.

Adult education.   Next is the trend toward more relevant ESL instruction at the adult level, where emphasis is being placed on job-related language. Too often in the past the ESL teacher has assumed that teaching English in a vacuum was his sole responsibility. Now it is becoming generally recognized that unless the content is relevant to the goals and life-choices of the students, the adult ESL program may be a disservice rather than an aid to them. Strategies being used include:

Selection or development of instructional materials using criteria of need and appropriateness of linguistic content and style

Role-playing activities (in place of often irrelevant dialogues) which allow students to acquire and practice English in anticipated contexts

On-the-job training in both English and job skills, sponsored by the industries or businesses hiring the non-English-speakers and emphasizing relevance and efficiency

All of these imply that teachers of English to adults must either commit themselves to learning about the content areas, or else that the teaching were better done by people who are themselves specialists in the content rather than in language teaching.

Study skills.   It has been recognized for some time that courses in English for foreign students at the university level frequently fall short of meeting graduates' needs. They have been left inadequately equipped with the skills they need for coping with university-level instruction in English. The need is for earlier and stronger emphasis on reading processes, and for teaching the more formal style required by textbooks and lectures rather than the conversational style often found in audio/lingual materials.

Strategies for meeting these needs include:

A shift in priorities to reading and writing

Courses and materials which teach subject-specific vocabulary

Instruction in using dictionaries and other reference aids

Placement of students in regular university courses as auditors prior to enrollment in a degree program, with concurrent assistance in interpreting textbooks, lectures, and tests

Graduate courses in research methods and writing style appropriate for American theses, dissertations, and comprehensive examinations

ESL methodology.   The most far-reaching change in the field is probably coming at the elementary and secondary levels with the recognition that language learning is most efficient when it is highly motivated by communication needs and when it is a medium for meaningful content. In other words, it is highly questionable how much learning is induced by the unmotivated pattern-practice exercises which often form the core of ESL instruction.

Related to this is the recognition that although we have theoretically known that learning strategies and interests as well as intellectual factors of children differ basically from those of adults, most of the ESL methods and materials now in use in our elementary and secondary classrooms represent relatively minor adaptations from those designed initially for adults. We must now go even further, however, and question whether these methods were ever really the most effective for adults.

Research on second language learning suggests that it progresses in many ways like first language learning, with the learner moving through a series of levels of mastery. It cannot be assumed that one structural form taught at one time will be acquired and used thereafter. Methods of teaching which require trial-and-error learning (as exemplified in the audio/lingual method) may be inappropriate for certain cultural groups— if not indeed for *all* cultural groups.

A second language is best taught not as an object in itself, but by using it as a medium to teach something else.

Integration.   We already have had serious reason to question homogeneous grouping of students for special ESL instruction because of motivational considerations. Not only are they likely to become victims of the negative expectations which are generated by such practices, but students will not learn the language itself as well under such circumstances as if it were being used to teach a content subject. Furthermore, they will not have the advantage of using English-speaking peers in the language learning classroom as models or as targets for *real* communication.

A frequent argument advanced in favor of such classes has been that specialized audio/lingual techniques and materials will foster the most efficient second language learning. If this proves to have been a poorly founded assumption, ESL teachers should be ready and anxious to try new methods. The logical alternative is *not,* however, to dump all non-English-speaking students into regular classes to sink or swim with teachers who have no understanding of their unique language problems and needs. Students with limited competence in English need *support instruction* in the English language which is directly related to and integrated with their English content instruction.

One alternative is to add an English support component to content classes in which there is a wide range of student language abilities. The purpose of such instruction is to:

Provide students with English labels and structures for the concepts they need to understand or wish to express

Assure that students can ask questions and understand answers

Provide students with positive support for the English that is being learned, without overcorrection of what has not yet been mastered

Guide and encourage students in the consistent addition of new linguistic forms

Assist students in learning how to learn and succeed in English, including initial or transfer reading instruction, and learning how to take tests (understanding the relative importance of time over correctness in our culture and the meaning of such specialized formats as "Fill in the blank" or "True or False")

Such support may be accomplished through a combination of educational strategies used in conjunction with English content instruction:

Informal and regular assistance from a content teacher who is additionally trained in second language methodology

Individualized activities which are either programmed for self-correction or accompanied by a cassette recording (e.g., sentences to be completed with a key word after hearing or reading a brief passage)

Cassette recordings of the written instructional material for students to listen to as they read along

Cassette recordings and/or written summaries of concepts presented in a lesson with controlled English vocabulary and structures

Such an English support program is quite compatible with the English content component of a bilingual curriculum but is perhaps most needed at the intermediate and secondary levels where keeping up with subject content is critical in both academic and social dimensions.

BASES FOR CHANGE

The recent trends listed in the preceding section follow naturally from experience and research which show us the importance of motivation and relevance in second language teaching. They also follow quite naturally from trends in such fields as special education to provide for so-called special needs in integrated classrooms. There is a trend as well among many minority communities throughout the country to strongly oppose traditional ESL pull-out classes for their children on constitutional grounds. They could probably succeed in proving that such programs are not giving students a maximal opportunity to learn, but schools should not wait for a court order to force change.

Eliminating special ESL classes would not by any means eliminate the need for TESL training (in fact, many more teachers with TESL training and interest would be required), but it would indeed call for some major changes in teacher preparation and in the materials being used.

While linguistics would still be very relevant in teacher training, educational methodology (such as how to teach reading and how to individualize instruction) would be central.

ESL-trained teachers would have to have something to teach—a content area on the secondary level, competencies for a self-contained classroom on the elementary one.

Teachers would need materials for individualized and small group instruction which were keyed to the content material of the standard curriculum and to students' language abilities.

While the TESL profession has made some progress over traditional forms of education in meeting the needs of bilingual students, there is no reason for it to be complacent. Now that the field is recognized and firmly established, there is a danger that members of the profession will spend their time defending a set of orthodox concepts and methods, rather than directing their energies toward meeting the actual needs and learning-styles of students or responding to the new directions indicated by research and experience in linguistics, psychology, anthropology, and education.

Changes are being instituted in classrooms across the country and around the world; at least the adaptations summarized in the following paragraphs are absolutely essential if TESL is to remain a vital force in the education of bilingual students.

It is essential to view non-English-speaking students positively, as already possessing skills in another language, as already well along in their conceptual development, and to use these resources as foundations upon which to build. The consequences of viewing and grouping students in terms of their relative "deficiencies" in English, their verbal "handi-caps" which require remediation, often extend Pygmalion-fashion to expectations of failure and projections of low esteem.

Also, it is important to perceive language and education in their cultural perspective. Linguistic differences among students and among communities are symptomatic of the differences in the broad scope of culture, of which language is only a part. Teachers must be sensitive to these differences and learn to appreciate and respect their expression, while at the same time teaching students to understand the culture of the United States which is expressed by the American English they are learning to speak.

Furthermore, English taught as a goal in itself, isolated from the curriculum, becomes an empty exercise devoid of meaning. Certainly at the elementary level, and perhaps at the secondary level as well, it would probably be best if there were no special ESL classes or teachers at all, but all teachers were trained in applying second language teaching methods in regular content-teaching.

Such changes require a willingness in the TESL field to assess honestly both progress and weaknesses, a willingness to adapt, and a willingness to learn. Unless its practitioners examine its methods and are prepared to change them, TESL as a profession may not maintain the status it has achieved in education, but become an anachronism which, like others, has failed. The challenge must be met if students' language-related needs are to be provided for—the purpose of TESL.

FOR ADDITIONAL READING

OLLER, JOHN W., JR. and JACK C. RICHARDS, eds., *Focus on the Learner: Pragmatic Perspectives for the Language Teacher* (Rowley, Mass.: Newbury House, 1973), especially Part VI: "Alternatives to Formal Language Instruction," pp. 265–301.

PAULSTON, CHRISTINA BRATT, "Linguistic and Communicative Competence," *TESOL Quarterly,* 8 (December 1974), 347–62.

RIVERS, WILGA R., "From Linguistic Competence to Communicative Competence," *TESOL Quarterly,* 7 (March 1973), 25–34.

SAVILLE-TROIKE, MURIEL, "TESOL Today: The Need for New Directions," *TESOL Newsletter,* 8 (November 1974); ERIC No. ED 096 833.

Survival Skills
for Students and Teachers

CHAPTER 6

If the field of TESL is in a period of change, if the adequacy of available ESL lessons must be questioned, then what is a teacher to do with students who speak little or no English? They cannot wait for research to answer our questions, for better textbooks to be written, nor even for additional personnel to be trained. They must learn English *now* if they are to survive in our educational and social system, and they must be taught. How?

GENERAL GUIDELINES

Give yourself and the students a chance.   As with every other aspect of human learning, enthusiasm and positive expectations enhance second language acquisition. If there is only one non-English-speaker or a handful in a class of native English-speakers, the non-native speaker(s) should *not* be sent off to "special" programs, no matter how attractive or logical these may seem. They will be helped more if they can be given English support instruction along with whatever else they study, and if they are kept with English-speaking peers. Dealing with non-English-speaking students in a heterogeneous classroom is just an extension of good practices in individualizing instruction.

Provide students with a desire to learn and opportunity for practice and reinforcement.   Much of the motivation for learning a language comes when that language is needed to communicate. This need is not only fostered by the heterogeneous assignment of students to classes, but by seating arrangements and grouping within the classroom which create the opportunity for students of varied language backgrounds to talk to each other, and group or committee assignments which create the need for them to do so. The greatest barrier to peer-reinforced language development is you-can-hear-a-pin-drop quiet, where no informal verbalization and communication are permitted. A noisy classroom is not desirable when study activities are underway, but quiet and natural talking may profitably accompany schoolwork.

Assign students by age.   Students should be assigned to classes according to appropriate age level, and not by measures of intelligence, language ability, or academic proficiency. This is true for the reasons of attitude, motivation, opportunity, and reinforcement given above. It is also true because tests, especially intelligence tests and achievement tests with norms set for English-speaking students, are completely unreliable when students are not fluent in English and have cultural experiences different from those presupposed in such testing contexts. Tests may be useful for evaluating teaching methods and materials, or for providing positive information on what skills and concepts you may be sure a student has acquired and upon which further instruction should be based, but you can never be sure the "missed" items are not due to the linguistic or cultural specificity of the test-makers, or to psychological factors potentially present in any alien and threatening situation. Students with limited English ability should never be burdened with the additional frustrations of time limits in the testing context. These restrictions serve no positive function, put students under needless additional pressure, and often prevent them from displaying what they know.

Don't think students are lacking in intelligence or treat them as if they were.   Even without scores on tests which often lend themselves to this misinterpretation, studies show that teachers unconsciously behave differently toward students who they think are disadvantaged. Teachers need to be aware of their own behavior, as well as bias in the methods they use. Several of the most widely adopted "compensatory" programs are based on the explicit assumption that students with different cultural and experiential backgrounds are deficient in concepts and in cognitive processes. The Pygmalion effect of negative expectations probably causes greater retardation of student achievement than any other single factor.

Don't overlook students with language needs. Students with limited English ability indeed have special needs and problems in school, even when they are being given adequate opportunities to hear and use the language. A student who feels inadequate in an English-speaking environment may withdraw as a defense against derision or failure, against being different. Or he may feel lost in an unintelligible world, or may tune out the strangeness around him. All are serious consequences requiring attention and aid, but "the squeaking hinge always gets the oil", and a very quiet and intentionally unobtrusive student may be overlooked. Numerous cases could be cited of students with "foreign" surnames whose severe hearing and pathological speech problems went undiagnosed through many months of school because their lack of speech was either not noticed or not considered abnormal. But even more often, normal students with inadequate English competence will be found who use silence or minimal responses to escape the individual attention which they need and deserve. Teachers need listening skills as much as students do.

Show acceptance and respect for cultural differences without stereotyping. There are very real cultural differences between different cultures in their food habits, family structure, values, attitudes, and means of expressing affection, grief, and embarrassment. Awareness of and respect for these differences is relevant to instructional methods, to the selection of appropriate teaching materials, and to the means used for classroom organization and control. Nevertheless, a teacher should never make the mistake of expecting students who share a similar background to be the same. While every group has its own distinctive cultural norms, there are always individual ranges of variation, and students are individuals. The teacher must be conscious of his own culture's traditional notions about other groups; it is only when such stereotypes are at a conscious level that we can free ourselves from them.

Use a variety of teaching techniques in a variety of learning contexts. Teaching students from diverse cultural backgrounds means teaching students with different styles of learning, students who have learned to learn in different ways. Teaching by a testing mode (trial-and-error, for instance) is inappropriate for many students who should not be asked to perform until they feel ready to do so successfully, and competition or other peer-challenge techniques are inappropriate for many more. Repetition and role-learning (for example, by means of recorded instructions that students may listen to over and over) may be helpful to some students in some contexts, but such caveats as "practice makes perfect" are not particularly necessary for language learning. Role-playing and simulation games are valuable media for instruction.

Emphasize communication of meaning instead of formal "correctness" in English. It is particularly important to remember during beginning language activities and in all levels of content instruction that the teacher's objective is to help students learn and verbalize concepts, not to correct their grammar or pronunciation. Students who find they do not use language acceptable to their teachers, especially in the early stages, often protect themselves by not talking any more than necessary when at school. Correction of speech patterns in communicative or expressive contexts can strongly inhibit the development of all language skills. Deviations from generally accepted forms made in these contexts may be unobtrusively noted and may guide the selection of usage practices in a more formal context for students who need it. Students will be greatly aided in learning English if the teacher gives instructions and explanations in consciously consistent patterns (using the same grammatical structures and vocabulary) until these are easily understood. Translation should be used whenever necessary and possible to clarify meaning.

Give students reasons to be proud of their native language and culture. The purpose of English instruction is *not* to replace the students' native language and culture. First, bilingualism is an asset; students should be encouraged to retain their own language and not abandon it for English. The student who is linguistically and culturally unique in a classroom is perhaps most vulnerable to pressures for assimilation. He can be helped in maintaining his pride and identity by recognizing him as a learning resource in the classroom, a student with wider experiences and information than the majority, and by encouraging further learning about his native language and culture. This is not in any way a barrier to Americanization.

Consider the whole student. It is being recognized increasingly that the school forms only a part of the student's total education, and that the family and community are an important part of this process. Effort should always be made to communicate with and involve parents in the formal educational process, but the home territory should not be invaded if school personnel are not welcome there. Insistence on entering every student's home is as ethnocentric as never leaving the school grounds. Some parents must be reached through alternative channels.

Many parents who are new in an area, or long-time residents who do not communicate in its dominant language, are not aware of available school and community health resources and need to be advised. This, too, is the school's responsibility. Parents also need to be informed about what happens to their children at school and made to feel welcome visiting classes or participating in such organizations as the PTA.

Considering the whole student also includes considering such details as what he gets to eat and what social influences and pressures he is under at recess and when school dismisses for the day. The guideline in instruction or intervention is maintaining the student's individual and group identity and self respect. The student with little or no facility in English is as much a human individual as any other, and as much deserving of care, respect, and success.

PRIORITIES

There are many things students need to know if they are to survive and succeed in an educational system in which a foreign language (English) is the chief medium of instruction. There is not time for everything; choices must be made and priorities determined.

Passive versus active: speaking versus writing. The passive skills, those required in decoding messages—listening and reading—are the most important language skills for the acquisition of knowledge. The active skills—speaking and writing—are required in normal learning contexts to a lesser degree, but frequently perform an informal testing function as student achievement level and progress are evaluated. Formal testing is more often also dependent on reading skill.

When survival in an English-dominant learning context is the objective, listening and reading skills are most critical for success. Speaking is especially important in a social dimension, but the non-English-speaking student already has expressive ability in another language which is much more appropriate in any case to use with the people who are closest to him. He will receive extensive exposure to spoken English if he is among English-speaking peers, but opportunities to learn reading and writing skills may well be limited to classroom instruction time.

Reading is probably the single most important skill for survival in our educational system, but one which has been woefully neglected in much traditional ESL instruction. The belief has been held that listening and speaking had to precede written language skills, but this was based on a fallacious analogy with the order of acquisition of skills for young children learning their first language. The process is not the same.

A student who already knows how to read in one language will not have to learn how to read all over again. If his language is closely related to English, as is Spanish or German, there will be almost complete transfer of reading ability. Even if his language is entirely unrelated to English and uses a different writing system, such as Chinese or Arabic, the essential process involved in decoding abstract symbols remains the same and is readily transferred in learning to read English.

The student with limited English who begins his initial reading in English should not have to wait until he has developed oral proficiency in the language, as is sometimes suggested. In the first place, learning to read is much too important for other learning and for school survival to be delayed; furthermore, multisensory input (both listening and reading) speeds and reinforces the process of acquiring English. The teacher must be conscious, however, of the differences involved in teaching reading to native speakers and to second language learners.

Pronunciation, grammar, or vocabulary.   The relative priority of these components of language must also be reconsidered when the objective is student survival in the English-dominant school. The audio/lingual method, most commonly used for ESL instruction in the last decade or two, stressed complete mastery of phonology as the initial objective and then learning all of the basic grammatical patterns with only a very limited vocabulary. It was felt that new words should be added *after* the basic structures were acquired.

For students learning and attempting to survive in a second language, that is not appropriate advice. Vocabulary is *most* important for understanding—knowing names for things, actions, and concepts. We can appeal to our common sense and experience in making this decision about priorities. Many of us have gotten along in foreign countries, even shopping, getting directions, and traveling in buses and taxis, if we just knew the names of what we wanted although we had no idea how to structure grammatical utterances. We could have had no such success with basic grammatical constructions, even flawlessly pronounced, if we had not had words in that language for the things we needed to express.

This is not to suggest that grammar and pronunciation are not important for students to learn—only that it is vocabulary that they need *first* in order to survive. English speakers can usually tolerate a great deal of diversity in pronunciation and grammar and still "get the message." Students even with little facility in English can express very complex concepts ungrammatically and still be understood, in part because of the high degree of redundancy in English sentences. And there is seldom any misunderstanding because a phonemic distinction is missed, at least when words occur in context and not in artificial minimal-pair drills. *Shoe* and *chew*, *share* and *chair*, *bit* and *beet* are rarely critical contrasts for English meaning, despite the time textbooks and curricula for Spanish-speaking students may spend on them.

A second decision about priorities must be made *within* the area of vocabulary, since there is a practical limit to the rate and number of words that can readily be taught and mastered. Differences in rate will depend to a great extent on how many cognates are shared between the student's native language and English. The vocabulary to teach first is the vocabulary the students need to know. This will insure motivation to learn it and opportunities for repetition and reinforcement. In particular, vocabulary development should be closely correlated with students' language needs in their content subjects.

Language style.   When the objective is survival, there is also a question of what style or variety of English is immediately needed by students. If they are in secondary school or college, this must be the more formal language of textbooks and lectures, and not the conversational style commonly found in audio/lingual materials. Students living in bilingual communities will continue to use their native language in informal contexts with family and friends, and students interacting with English-speaking peers will have many opportunities to learn the informal variety on the playground, after school, and from movies and television. But they have only class time in which to learn the variety they need for school, and for more formal social contexts. While they must of course learn to understand informal speech, given limited time, the emphasis must be on developing control of formal written and spoken English.

There is seldom any need for children to understand or use a more formal style of English during their elementary school years, and thus it has lower priority at that level, but they should probably be exposed to it in the receptive dimension to enhance their chances for later academic success.

WHAT TO DO WHEN ...

Beyond general guidelines for classroom practices and for deciding on priorities in English teaching, few specific recommendations can be made without reference to particular language learning contexts. For this purpose, it will be useful to look at some of the more typical classroom situations in the United States which require teaching English as a second language and to consider suggestions for methods and appropriate procedures.

Situation.

The first day of school finds a kindergarten class in which one-third of the children understand no English at all, one-third have limited facility in it, and one-third are fluent or native speakers of English.

SUGGESTIONS:

1. The native languages of every child should be used to the greatest extent possible for at least the initial welcoming and orientation to school procedure. The first day of school is often the most traumatic in a student's life, particularly if he does not know English. Even a few words and phrases will help set an accepting environment for each child and his language and culture.

2. Help (paid or volunteer) should be enlisted from one or more adults or older students who can communicate with the non-English-speaking children. If the school cannot afford to hire a permanent bilingual aide, such assistance for even the first few days of school will help children through the initial period of adjustment.

3. Name tags should be prepared in advance with addresses and/or bus instructions and pinned on each child for at least the first week. Over half of these children would not be able to tell an English-speaking bus' driver or traffic patrolman where they lived. Parents in many cultures do not use a child's official "school" name in address, so he may not even recognize it. Name tags should also include the name he is really called.

4. Toys and realia which will be familiar to children from different cultural groups represented should be included in the classroom, so that everything is not new and strange all at once. Records of songs or stories in whatever languages the children speak are probably available on loan from the public library or may be purchased.

5. Children should be encouraged to verbalize (in any language) about what they are doing. The non-English-speaking students should soon be provided some English labels for objects and events in the classroom, but not immediately, and never in a tone which discourages the use of another language.

Situation.

It is early in the school year in a first grade class in which there are two children who have had no prior experience with school or with English, ten more who have learned some English in kindergarten but are still not fluent, and the rest who are fluent or native speakers of English.

SUGGESTIONS:

1. When there are enough children in other first grade classes in the school who speak little or no English, the practice is often followed of putting them in a single classroom together (frequently called a pre-first or beginners' class, with the expectation that they will be placed in a regular first grade the following year). *This is not recommended.* They will have much less opportunity to learn English than they would if kept with English-speaking students, and no opportunity at all to participate in the "normal" age and grade sequence, either socially or academically. Such administrative retardation has no justification from the point of view of language learning, it helps create feelings of defeat and failure and behavior problems, and it may additionally result in eventual withdrawal from school.

2. Two "buddies" can be assigned to each of the two new students: one who speaks his language and a little English and one monolingual English speaker. Allow the trio to sit together, to work together on any assignments, and to talk quietly to one another during work periods. This arrangement will allow the two new students to feel some sense of security in the new situation, insure that some meaning accompanies classroom procedures, and provide some early opportunity for success. The two children with limited English will learn much more of it as they interpret the teacher's and the English-speaking child's words and the school context for the new students, and will have the additional positive experience of switching the usual prestige factor. The child becomes the teacher, and he has more knowledge than the culturally dominant student.

3. Both group and individualized teaching strategies can be used (as illustrated later in this chapter) to teach additional English skills to the non-English-speakers and limited-English-speakers. Priority should be given to providing English labels for objects and activities in school, critical vocabulary for social studies, science, and arithmetic topics, the forms of common directions and questions, and initial reading and writing skills.

Situation.

First grade has begun in an area where almost all of the children come from a similar language background and all are learning English as a second language (as in some Bureau of Indian Affairs schools, or in regions heavily populated by a single ethnic minority that is choosing to retain its language and culture).

SUGGESTIONS:

1. These children would profit most from bilingual education. While other more heterogeneous groups may also benefit from bilingual

instruction, a group such as this has little chance for an adequate education without it. Where there is little immediate need for English for communicative purposes and few peer models who speak it natively, students lack the motivations, opportunities, and reinforcements needed to lead to a control of English sufficient for success in a monolingual English program.

2. An important necessity is a teacher from the children's own ethnic group who speaks the children's language fluently and is trained to teach in it. Lacking this combination of competencies, ethnic identity and language fluency are the most important characteristics, since provision for training can be made by the school. An aide who speaks the children's language can be assigned to work with a monolingual English teacher, but this has the undesirable effect of perpetuating a role model distinction for the children, and should be avoided.

3. There should be no rush in this case to introduce reading and writing in English, since these skills should be taught first in the children's native language. Attempts to teach reading in both languages at once may cause interference.

4. English vocabulary and basic sentence patterns should be introduced which relate to objects and experiences in the school environment, and at least one content area (probably arithmetic or science) should be taught through the medium of English. When English is used, a conscious effort should be made to keep instruction and explanations in a consistent form. If the pattern *Two plus two equals four* is used one time, it should be used consistently, e.g., *Three plus three equals six*, and not varied as *Three and three are six* or *Three added to three gives you six*. Such equivalent structures are usually not learned until children are well along in their second language acquisition and add needless linguistic confusion (especially when the primary objective of a lesson is to teach arithmetic). A paraphrase form should only be added when there is no new cognitive information, and when the equivalence is overtly drawn or explained in translation.

5. Children's grammar or pronunciation in English or any other language should not be corrected when they are trying to communicate something in it.

Situation.

In a fourth grade class in an agricultural area during harvest season, half of the students are children of migrant laborers who will be moving on to another area within a few weeks.

SUGGESTIONS:

1. Students on the migrant circuit usually have a very predictable pattern of school attendance (and absence) from season to season and

year to year. School districts that share the same students need excellent intercommunication channels if the students are to receive consistent and efficient instruction. The schools should make an effort to provide as much commonality in curriculum organization and textbook selection as is possible across district and state boundaries.

2. Content is best organized into units or modules in which all subjects are immediately interrelated, and which provide culminating experiences at least once a month.

3. Packets of lessons and reading material should be prepared which can be sent along with students as they move. The help of older brothers and sisters or parents in continuing the students' education as the family moves can be enlisted, or a game format can be used which might be attractive and feasible during the travel period ahead.

4. Up-to-date résumés of student work should be kept and sent with them to the next teacher. Many migrant parents feel, often justifiably, that their children will not receive equal attention from teachers if their travel plans are known, so some way of gaining parental confidence is necessary. Written notes, whether in English or in the parents' native language, are usually ineffective. The migrant community has its own social structure, and identifying and communicating with its leaders is usually the most productive procedure.

Situation.

A sixth grade class in an ethnically mixed neighborhood of a port-of-entry city has thirty students, of whom seven speak English natively (although some perhaps only a nonstandard variety) and the other twenty-three speak ten different languages among them and have varying degrees of proficiency in English.

SUGGESTIONS:

1. As much information as possible should be collected about the educational background of each student. They will have had very diverse experiences, and to provide adequately for such diversity it is necessary to know which are literate in their native language, which have had schooling only in English, what other school systems they have attended, and what their previous experience means in terms of subjects studied and levels attained. There is great divergence among countries in curricular content and organization, and many of them are ahead of the United States.

2. Every port-of-entry city should request textbooks and other information from countries represented for a curriculum center, and have a curriculum specialist who can help interpret other educational systems to teachers with immigrant students. Such a center can also distribute

appropriate instructional materials received from other countries for teachers to use in individualizing content instruction and allowing these students to continue their cognitive development. Books for extensive reading requested from the countries of student origin will also help students who are literate in their native languages to maintain and improve these skills.

3. A high priority should be put on developing skills in reading and writing English. For students with very limited English at least, it is usually better to teach vocabulary from the content subjects in reading, writing, and oral language activities rather than to add an additional vocabulary and structure load from so-called reading texts per se.

4. Summaries of the content of lessons in the various subject areas should be prepared in simplified English or be translated into the ten dominant languages of the students for supplementary review. For a student not literate in his native language, someone from the same community (perhaps an older family member) can be asked to tape record the translations for his use.

5. Students should be encouraged to work together in small groups on most assignments, and quiet talk should be allowed during work periods. English will be the lingua franca for this class and thus will tend to be used even for social interchange, but students should never be discouraged from using their native language with others in the class who might share it.

6. Sensitivity is required for the many problems these students may be having in a strange country, and for the conflicts that may develop between them and their parents as new values, beliefs, and behaviors are encountered and perhaps tried out. English classes for parents may be arranged to help reduce the gap between home and school. Since there are structural and cultural as well as curricular differences between school systems, recent arrivals (both students and parents) may need orientation on how their new one operates.

Situation.

An eighth grade class in remedial reading is composed of fifteen students from bilingual homes. All have been in a monolingual English educational program for at least eight years and communicate in English, but none have acquired functional reading skills or seem very anxious to learn at this stage.

SUGGESTIONS:

1. The vicious cycle of failure, low motivation, and negative expectations must be broken for these students. More of the same kind of instruction they have had will probably not work. One approach would

be to try teaching them to read in their native language instead of English. This will have a number of potential advantages: it is different and therefore more likely to capture their attention and interest; they have not acquired a history of failure at the task; it may be considered more prestigious in their social reference group; and the language probably has more regular sound-symbol correspondences (unless it is Chinese), which may make it easier to acquire some basic word attack skills, which would transfer later to English.

2. A variety of reading material should be used, depending on student interest and responsiveness. Often available is controlled reading material prepared for this age level in first and second year foreign language classes, but comic books, newspapers, magazines, and paperbacks may also be available in communities with large bilingual populations.

3. The school or neighborhood librarian should be asked for lists of holdings in the students' language or requested to order some if they are not now available.

4. If there is a bilingual program underway in the district at the primary level, these older students can collect, write, or translate stories for the children. The change in roles and models could be very beneficial for both groups.

5. Under no circumstances should either English or native language pronunciation and grammar be "corrected" if remedial students are reading aloud; spelling or grammar should not be corrected if they are writing (unless it is a story to be used for younger children). Such niceties can be worried about only after fluency and feeling of success are solidly established.

Situation.

A tenth grade student enrolls in classes composed entirely of native English-speakers. He was very successful in the school system which he left but knows no English at all.

SUGGESTIONS:

1. Before deciding on priorities in this case, the parents' plans must be determined. If they are on temporary assignment here and plan to return to their home country for the remainder of their child's education, his needs would be quite different from those he would have if they were immigrants and the remainder of his education, perhaps including college, would be in English. In the latter case, the main need is learning to learn in English. In the former, positive social experiences with United States students and learning about United States culture may well be most important.

2. An immediate need in any case is for some basic words and phrases in English. Some programmed material for teaching English as a foreign language would be appropriate initially. Contextual relevance in dialogues and exercises, focusing on a school setting and vocabulary rather than on shopping or ordering meals, should be the primary criterion for selection.

3. The student should attend a couple of solid content classes taught in English even during his first semester, but should also have some less formal classes which will be more conducive to social interaction and require less concentrated effort and need in English. He might include physical education, shop, art, or music, depending on his interests. Instead of the regular English class, he should be assigned for that period to one teacher for an English support tutorial. Such special instruction should generally be limited to one semester, after which his needs should be met through individualized attention in regular classes.

4. English instruction during the tutorial should be immediately relevant to the content courses the student is taking. If a text or workbook in English as a foreign language is being used (and these generally are *not* immediately relevant), the tutor should provide auxiliary explanation and exercises using the vocabulary of the content course, for instance. With the understanding and cooperation of the teachers of the content courses, the language tutor should substitute more appropriate assignments for those given the class (but on the same topics), and feel free to give all assistance needed for their successful completion.

5. Tutoring or supplementary instructional material on the same content topics should also be made available in the student's native language. His parents may be willing and able to provide this themselves with guidance and cooperation from the school.

6. Grades based on performance compared with native English-speakers would be absolutely meaningless, but might prevent his acceptance to college a few years from now. Credits which do not count in a grade point average for at least the first year would be a reasonable alternative at the administrative level.

Situation.

A freshman composition class in a small college has no special language program for foreign students. One is enrolled in this class. He understands his lectures and textbooks in other classes (with only a little difficulty), but makes many errors in choosing prepositions, articles, and verb forms.

SUGGESTIONS:

1. Help for this student should concentrate on writing English. His exact language needs depend in part on what subject area he is

majoring in, how his other professors feel about correctness or form versus content in written assignments and tests, and what his future educational and career plans are, but he certainly should develop a writing style which more closely approximates standard English. We have far less tolerance for variation in written English than we do in speech, especially in a fairly formal academic context.

2. A description contrasting his language with English should be secured, or a grammatical description of his language. Studying it may help to clarify why certain deviations from English norms occur in his writing, and may help suggest strategies for overcoming these.

3. The student's language problems should be discussed with his other instructors (in part to insure their understanding of the nature and cause of his errors—the fact that for him English is a foreign language). They should know he will be receiving help to overcome his difficulties. With their permission, the student should be assisted with the mechanics of his English in assignments for other courses and allowed to correct errors in form before handing them in to other teachers. He should be given credit in the English course for these same assignments.

4. Not all errors should be corrected at once, or the student will be overwhelmed with red ink. At first, only articles should be corrected (when to use *the, a,* or nothing) and written exercises should be provided which drill this aspect of grammar. After this has improved considerably, his choice of prepositions can be corrected and exercises given which focus on these; then correction and explanation of troublesome verb forms can be added.

5. He should purchase a dictionary and a reference grammar or freshman handbook and be guided in learning to use these to check his own work in each area of focus.

Situation.

An evening high school equivalency class is composed of both adult immigrants and native-born high school dropouts who want more formal education or have found they need it. Competence levels in English range from near zero to fluency.

SUGGESTIONS:

1. The first step is to find out why each student is there and what he wants and expects to learn. These students have all probably already put in a hard day's work, and they are likely to lose interest or consider the class a waste of time if their own needs and expectations are not provided for, or alternative motivation cultivated.

2. All basic subjects (mathematics, history, etc.) are content for ESL instruction, and there should be no artificial separation of language and content in courses, instructors, or materials. Translation and support in the students' native language should be utilized whenever it contributes to concept development and characterization.

3. English instruction, especially vocabulary acquisition, should also be directly related to the vocational interests and needs of the students. Realistic contexts for language use should be emphasized, and dialogues and drills with no obvious relevance eliminated from the curriculum. Such language development techniques will be appropriate for both native speakers and non-English-speaking students as long as vocational relevance and realism are strictly maintained.

4. The positive value of bilingual competence for the secretary, nurse, teacher, doctor, and lawyer (and their aides) must not be overlooked, and provisions should be made for the bilingual students' continued native language development in vocational and professional areas such as these. Provisions should minimally include increment of vocabulary, literacy training, and development of the standard language form and style.

This chapter has presented a number of global procedures and guidelines for the teacher working in a variety of contexts with students with no command of English or only a limited command. Although the classroom is not the only, or perhaps even the major, arena in which learning takes place, we are only beginning to realize how much effect the teacher can have in facilitating or inhibiting learning there. Sensitivity and concern are the most important characteristics a teacher can have, but without knowledge and understanding there is a limit to what these qualities can achieve. At the same time, a set of techniques mechanically applied will not produce automatic results. We must remember that language is a human characteristic, and above all we must approach its teaching humanely.

FOR ADDITIONAL READING

SAVILLE-TROIKE, MURIEL, "Basing Practice on What We Know about Children's Language," in *Classroom Practices in ESL and Bilingual Education*, Vol. 1 (Washington, D.C.: Teachers of English to Speakers of Other Languages, 1973), pp. 1–9; ERIC No. ED 093 156.

Strategies
for Instruction

CHAPTER 7

Learning a second language requires a variety of psychological and social conditions, including motivation, attention, the availability of appropriate linguistic models, and both the need and the opportunity to use the target language in real communicative situations. To provide for these conditions activities for second language instruction will have to differ in several respects from the activities utilizing audio/lingual materials still typically used in special ESL classes. Most important perhaps is that the vocabulary to be included in the activities must be essentially determined by the content areas the students are studying in English. A second critical difference will be the inclusion of native English-speakers in the same activities to provide peer models and real communicative contexts for the second language learners, and a third will be a shift of primary focus to expressing or understanding a concept, with only secondary concern for formal correctness.

All of the sample language activities listed below are designed to be used for heterogeneous groups of students (including one or more students with limited facility in English and some native speakers), or to provide individualized English support instruction for students who need it in conjunction with their regular content instruction. Group activities therefore include language experiences appropriate for different levels of English proficiency and content or recreational features of interest and value to students not needing the language instruction. Individual activities should be related to the English language needs of students in such content areas as science, social studies, and mathematics.

These activities represent a distillation of practices which have been tested successfully in classroom use, but they do not constitute ESL lessons in themselves. They are intended to be samples of types of strategies for adapting regular content and teaching methods to the needs of students with only limited English. The heaviest emphasis in the activities given here is on teaching English to younger students, in kindergarten or the primary grades, because most students learning English as a second language in the United States first encounter the language at this level.

Activities are given below in the following order of focus: vocabulary development, grammar, pronunciation, reading, writing, listening, speaking, and other dimensions of communication.

VOCABULARY DEVELOPMENT

Young children. The primary goals for vocabulary development in young children are to provide English labels for things and concepts they have already learned in their first language, new concepts and labels which build on these, and categories with English labels for organizing these concepts efficiently.

Group activities.

TO TEACH NAMES OF OBJECTS:

1. Put several objects of different colors, shapes, and sizes on a table in front of the children, naming each one as you do so. Until you are sure most know all of the nouns, point to one object at a time and ask, *What is this?* (Ask children you think know the words first, so that they provide a model for the others to learn from.)

2. Have the children close their eyes while you put one object out of sight behind your back. Ask, *What is in my hand?* The only necessary response is the noun that names the object. Let several children take turns hiding objects behind their backs and asking the others, *What is in my hand?*

3. Without removing it from the table, look at an object and say, *I see something. What is it?* The child who guesses is "it" and asks others to guess what he is looking at.

TO TEACH DESCRIPTIVE WORDS AND CATEGORY LABELS:

1. Touch each of the objects on the table and describe it by color, saying, *The (book) is (red).* Then ask, *What is (red)?* and *What color is*

the (book)? Remember that the English terms may not match the color categories in the students' native language.

Repeat, describing by shape (*long, round,* or *square*) or size (*big* or *little*). Then let children continue the guessing game, using color, shape, size, or any combination of these as clues. Again, remember that some of these categories may be different or absent in the students' native language.

2. Put the objects in a bag and let the children take turns reaching in without looking. Depending on language level, they might just name the object they feel, or they might describe it for others to guess.

Add more objects to be identified and described, including some with multiple colors or patterns and irregular shapes.

3. Show several pictures of people or things cut from magazines. Have the class decide whether they are *happy or sad, new or old,* or *hot or cold.* Have the children discuss why they decided on a label, if possible.

4. Have several children act out one of a given pair of words and let the others guess which they are portraying. Say *happy or sad,* and a child should either smile or frown. The others then guess and take turns with *new or old* or *hot or cold.* If this activity is successful, add other pairs, such as *short or tall* and *fast or slow.*

TO TEACH VERBS:

1. Demonstrate verb meanings to the class. Say, *I am walking,* while walking; *I am jumping,* while jumping, etc. Give the command forms (as, *Jump!*) to the whole class and all say together, *We are (jumping).* Repeat, with individual children or pairs of children giving commands and describing their actions.

2. Have the children close their eyes and one child perform some action, such as running, hopping, skipping, or jumping. By sound alone the others should guess what he is doing.

3. Have the children stand in a circle and roll or bounce a large ball to one another. Each child should describe his own action when he is rolling, bouncing, or catching the ball.

TO TEACH WORDS FOR COMPARISON AND CATEGORIZATION:

1. Use cookies to help teach the words and concepts *enough* and *not enough.* Let the children count how many are present, decide how many cookies are needed, and then eat them.

2. Put three items that go together (such as *chalk, a pencil* and *a pen*) on a table and add one that does not belong to the same category (such as *a stick*). Ask the children which does not belong and why. Repeat

with such groups as *cake, cookie, candy,* and *carrot,* or *book, magazine, newspaper,* and *block.* Be sure all of the items can be named in each case as an initial step in the activity.

3. Let children collect bottle caps and bring them to school to be counted and compared over a period of several days. Words like *more* and *fewer* should be used.

Individual activities.

TO TEACH NAMES OF OBJECTS:

1. As children are coloring, painting, or looking at books, encourage them to name the objects or people in the pictures.

2. Put strips of masking tape on the floor to represent rungs on a ladder, and place an object on each. Children "climb" the ladder by naming the object on each step. Let them replace the objects with others for themselves or another child to name.

3. Leave all of the objects that were introduced during the group activities available to the children for individual exploration or for "playing school" in pairs or trios, as they wish.

TO TEACH DESCRIPTIVE WORDS AND CATEGORIES:

1. Have precut circles and squares of different colors available for individual use on a flannelboard or on a desk top. Children may group them by shape and then regroup according to color, or they may make designs with any desired combination. The final arrangement might be pasted on a piece of paper if they wish to preserve it. Ask individuals to name the colors and shapes, or to describe their designs.

2. Have children sit two by two on the floor, back to back. Both children in the pair should be given strings with a large knot tied in one end and identical sets of unstrung beads (the preschool variety which have different colors and shapes). As one child puts the beads on the string, he describes each one in order: *square red bead, round yellow bead,* etc. The second child follows these directions without looking at the first child's string. When finished, they match strings to see if the beads are in the same order, and then repeat with the second child giving directions.

Pairs of children may try more complicated descriptions by trying to match constructions with blocks, clay figures, designs made with precut shapes. Or each may just begin with a piece of drawing paper and a box of crayons and try to make the same pictures or designs from verbal descriptions alone.

TO TEACH VERBS:

Take photographs of children doing different things in the class-room or on the playground, such as painting, sitting, swinging, washing their hands, or eating. Let the children pictured show the photographs to others and tell what they are doing in the pictures.

TO TEACH WORDS FOR COMPARISON AND CATEGORIZATION:

1. Give two or three children several small circles cut from different colors of construction paper, a sheet of drawing paper, and some paste. After they have each pasted a number of the circles on the paper, ask such questions as: *Do you have more red circles or more blue circles? Who has the most yellow circles? Who has the fewest green circles?*

2. Let children cut pictures from a mail-order catalogue, and then sort them into categories for their own "wish book." They should think up titles they want printed at the top of each page (by the teacher or aide), such as *Clothes, Toys,* or *Furniture.* The categorization might also be done by function, such as *Things to Wear* and *Things to Play With.*

3. Use informal opportunities to point out *This is bigger than that,* or to use other comparatives when their meaning will be clear from the context.

Older students. The primary goals of vocabulary development activities for older students are to teach the meanings of the English terms they hear or read in all subject areas, to introduce English conceptual categories (and labels) which differ from those in the students' native languages, to generally decrease feelings of strangeness about the language, and to teach skills for independently finding the meaning of new words.

Group activities.

TO TEACH MEANING FOR WORDS IN CONTENT SUBJECTS:

1. Read sentences and longer passages from science or social studies books, leaving out an occasional word. Have students supply the missing words. This may be a written assignment, with blank spaces left for missing words or phrases. Although this is a group activity, students will be able to respond successfully at a variety of levels.

2. Referring to objects mentioned in the textbook, say, *I'm thinking of something that is _____ and _____.* Continue giving clues until students guess what the object is.

3. Put the previous activity into a "Twenty Questions" format.

Students ask questions to determine what is being thought of, and should only answer *yes* or *no*.

4. Call attention to new words that have recently been borrowed into or coined in English. Explain sources for names of new inventions, discoveries, products, and new institutions or organizations. Interesting types to consider are *portmanteau words* (motor + hotel = motel; smoke + fog = smog) and *acronyms* (UNESCO; NATO).

TO TEACH ENGLISH CONCEPTUAL CATEGORIES:

List a number of terms that belong to a single subject area and have the class arrange them in hierarchical order (a taxonomy). For instance, terms in a health lesson might include *food, meat, milk, dairy products, vegetables, carrots, beef, lamb, radishes, lettuce, cheese, eggs,* and *celery.* These would be categorized as by the accompanying diagram:

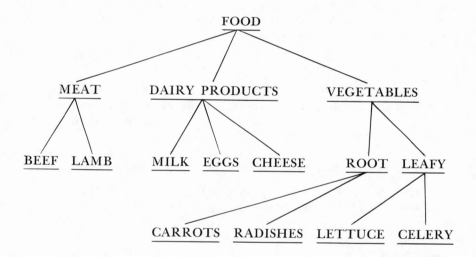

A similar format would be appropriate for lists of plants or animals, geographical features, modes of transportation, etc.

TO DECREASE FEELINGS OF "STRANGENESS" ABOUT THE LANGUAGE:

1. If any students in the class speak a language which is related to English (such as Spanish, German, or French), have the group look for *cognates,* or words in the two languages that have a common origin. An etymological dictionary would be useful in this assignment.

2. Have students look for words in English which have been borrowed from another language. Such languages need not be related, but may indicate cultural contacts of various kinds, from trade to conquest.

In addition to contributing to English vocabulary development, such activities document the close cultural ties between speakers of the two languages, and place the bilingual students in an advantageous position in contributing to a class assignment.

Individual activities.

TO TEACH MEANING FOR WORDS IN CONTENT SUBJECTS:

1. Have every student maintain a notebook of words which are new to him and which he thinks he may want to use in the future. The entry form that is generally easiest and clearest for second language learners consists of one or more examples of the word in context plus a simpler paraphrase in English, or a translation into the learner's native language (if he can read and write it).

2. Whenever possible, translate for students any new English words they encounter and cannot understand. Teach literate students how to use a bilingual dictionary and make sure that one is available for each language represented in the class.

TO TEACH ENGLISH CONCEPTUAL CATEGORIES:

Have students list vocabulary items for a single subject area on 3×5 index cards and arrange them as appropriate into contrastive sets (at the same level of abstraction) or into hierarchies. Students should be guided and corrected by a native English-speaker.

TO DECREASE FEELINGS OF "STRANGENESS" ABOUT THE LANGUAGE:

Have students individually compile lists of words that they hear or read which have been borrowed into English from their native language.

GRAMMAR

Young children. The primary goals of grammar instruction for young children are to teach noun and verb inflections, prepositions, and question, command, and negative forms of simple sentences.

Group activities.

TO TEACH NOUN INFLECTIONS:

1. Use some of the same objects introduced in vocabulary development activities to teach plural and possessive forms in English.

2. Review the objects' names and introduce the plural by pointing to two or more of the same objects and asking, *What are these?* Again, ask English-speakers first so that they can provide a model for the appropriate response. Combine the names of objects with descriptive words, as, *The (books) are (red)*, and use the patterns in similar comparative and categorical constructions, as you did for vocabulary development.

3. The possessive form should be introduced in relation to the children's names and to objects that they possess (as, *That is Mary's shoe*, or *This is Bill's picture*) instead of in more artificial activities where children don't really possess the objects and have to give things back.

TO TEACH VERB INFLECTIONS:

1. Continue the demonstration and participation activities that were used to introduce verb meanings in vocabulary development. Say, *I am going to walk* (or, *I will walk*), *I am walking* (while walking), and then, *I walked* (after having stopped). Repeat with other verbs, having the whole class, individuals, or pairs of children describe their actions. Guessing-activities may also be incorporated.

2. Put toy animals in a box and pretend they are asleep. Have one child tiptoe to the box and "wake" an animal. He says, *The _____ was sleeping.* He may then make the animal jump, run, or walk while another child says, *The _____ is _____ing.* That child may then "wake" another animal.

3. Call on one child and ask, *What are you going to do?* He should say one sentence describing what he is going to do, such as, *I am going to jump*, or, *I am going to run fast.* He then does what he has said he would do, and then says, *I jumped*, or, *I ran fast.* Repeat the activity until most of the children have had a turn.

TO TEACH PREPOSITIONS:

1. Combine prepositional phrases with verbs in their various forms and with nouns that have been learned, again beginning with demonstration and participation activities, for example, *I am walking to the door, John hopped to the table, Pete is standing on the block, Mary is sitting under the desk.*

2. Put an empty box upside down on the table together with some of the objects the children know by name and put one object under it, saying, *The (book) is under the box.* Have children place other objects *in, on, under,* or *beside* the box and describe the location of the objects as they do so.

3. Place a variety of objects in the box. Let children take turns choosing an item from the box as they say, *A _____ is in the box.* They

then put the object anywhere in the room and describe its location (on the table, under the desk, behind the piano).

Repeat, with each child choosing two items and saying, *A* _____ *and a* _____ *are in the box.* They then place the objects around the room and describe their locations.

TO TEACH QUESTION, COMMAND, AND NEGATIVE FORMS:

1. Give two or three commands in a series to the class or to individuals; for example, *Walk to the table, stand on the chair, and then sit under the table,* or, *Hop to the door and then skip to the window.* Let children take turns giving such commands to one another.

2. Have one child "place" himself in the room (on a chair, under a table). Ask *Where is* _____? and let other children describe his location. Change to a *who*-completion-question, such as *Who is under the table?* Place blocks, balls, and other objects around the room. Ask about each, *What is on/in/under the* _____? *Where is/are the* _____? Have children take turns asking the questions as well as answering.

3. Give a command to one child, such as *Mary, take a chair to the door,* or, *Freddie, take a block to Joe.* That child should then give a command and so on until each one has given and followed a command. Encourage each child to think of a different command.

4. Have one child cover his eyes or leave the room briefly while a second child performs some action in front of the class. The child who is "it" asks the class *Did he* _____? The class answers *Yes, he* _____, or, *No, he didn't* _____. After three incorrect guesses the class tells the person who is "it" the answer and another child is chosen to continue the game.

Individual activities.

TO TEACH NOUN INFLECTIONS:

Ditto pictures including certain single objects and sets of two or more of the same objects, for example, a picture of a girl eating an apple and a picture of two girls eating apples. Instruct children to *Circle the (apple)* and, *Circle the (apples).* Let children work in small groups of two or three and give directions to one another.

TO TEACH VERB INFLECTIONS:

Have children draw pictures of something they did the day before (or something they want to do tomorrow) and dictate a description of it for us to write at the bottom. Write the standard verb form if they have given an incorrect form and read it back with the revision, but do not otherwise correct the children's stories.

TO TEACH PREPOSITIONS:

1. Provide a very large box for the children to climb *into, on, under,* or *around* and have them describe their own actions or locations.

2. Tape record series of directions for individual children to use in drawing or assembling a design, leaving time for them to follow each direction after it is given. For example, you may tell them to *Draw a red circle; draw a blue square beside the red circle; draw a yellow triangle under the blue square.* Have a copy of the design specified in each set of directions for children to match with their results.

Older students. Older students must be able to process the more complex grammatical structures that are common to textbooks at their level, and they should know how and where to use modifiers, conjunctions, and subordinators to expand their own sentences.

Group activities.

TO TEACH COMPLEX STRUCTURES:

1. Give students two or more sentences to combine in a variety of ways. For example, students might be given the simple sentences:

I have a dog.
My dog is brown.
My dog is big.
My dog eats a lot.

Possible student responses are (in order of increasing complexity):

I have a dog. He is brown and big. He eats a lot.
I have a dog that is big and brown. He eats a lot.
I have a big brown dog, and he eats a lot.
I have a big brown dog that eats a lot.

More advanced students should understand that the different combinations may not be exactly equivalent in meaning.

2. Write a sentence on the board and have students list shorter sentences which are included in its meaning. For instance, *Jack and Jill went up the hill* includes the concepts (assertions):

Jack went up the hill.
Jill went up the hill.

The boy that I saw is short and fat includes:

> *I saw a boy.*
> *The boy is short.*
> *The boy is fat.*

3. Grammatical signals are perhaps best brought into focus as answers to questions: *What did they do? How many did it? Where? When?* Until students can respond without hesitation, such questions should be based on assertions or declarative sentences (oral or written) in active voice; for example, *Many students were at the movie yesterday,* and *The boy read the book.* Common inversions should then be added in the question drills, with questions based on similar sentences with adverb initial or passive construction; for example, *Yesterday many students were at the movie; There were many students at the movie yesterday; The book was read by the boy.*

TO TEACH SENTENCE EXPANSIONS:

Begin with a simple sentence and ask students to squeeze additional information into it. The content should relate to subjects being studied. For instance:

> Initial sentence:
> *The Mississippi is a river.*
> Additional information:
> *Where is it? How big is it?*
> Possible final sentence:
> *The Mississippi, which flows from Minnesota to Louisiana, is the largest river in the United States.*

Individual activities.

TO TEACH COMPLEX STRUCTURES:

1. Write long words on strips of paper and have students cut them apart into smaller units which still have meaning (smaller words, prefixes, or suffixes). New words can be made by combining parts of the originals.

2. The processing of complex sentences can be guided with questions (*Who? What? Where? When? How?*), and students should be taught to use this procedure independently, as well as in the question activities suggested above for the group.

3. Tape record summaries of important content in simplified English structures or in native language translation so that students can

check their understanding of the concepts presented in the complex sentences. Brief self-checking quizzes in simplified English or translation can serve much the same purpose.

4. The teacher, aide, or tutor should then use a complex structure which has been misunderstood as the basis for one of the synthetic or analytic exercises described above under group or individual activities (putting simple sentences together and breaking complex sentences apart).

PRONUNCIATION

Young children. The primary goals in the development of second language pronunciation of young children are the aural discrimination and oral production of differences in sound which make a difference in word meanings (the *phonemic* distinctions in the language).

Group activities.

TO TEACH DISCRIMINATION BETWEEN /b/ AND /v/:

1. Give each child two flash cards, one with the letter *B* and one with the letter *V* printed on them. Say several words that begin with one or the other sound and have the children respond by holding up the card illustrating the initial consonant that matches that initial sound of the word.

2. On a flannelboard put pictures of children named Bob and Virginia (or other names beginning with *B* and *V*). Also have pictures of several objects designated by words that contain /b/ and several with /v/. The children should sort the pictures, putting all those with /b/ under Bob and all those with /v/ under Virginia.

TO TEACH DISCRIMINATION BETWEEN /š/ AND /č/:

1. Say several words containing both /š/ and /č/. Have the children respond by clapping softly or raising their hands when they hear /š/ (or they can put their fingers to their lips to indicate the "quiet" sound).

2. Put a *ch*air and a *sh*oe in front of the class. Hold up several objects designated by words that contain one sound or the other (*sh*ip, wat*ch*, di*sh*, *ch*ocolate, etc.) and have the children sort them—/č/'s on the *ch*air, and /š/'s in the *sh*oe.

To teach discrimination between /b/ and /v/:

1. Cut flower vases out of blue, black, and brown construction paper and place them in a box or bag. Have one child reach into the box or bag without looking and guess, *I have a (blue) vase.* If he guesses correctly, he gets another turn.

2. In a bag have pictures or objects whose names contain the sound /b/ or /v/. One child at a time should reach in and pull one out, saying, *I am taking a _____ from the bag.* This could also be played as a guessing game with each child saying *I think there is a _____ in the bag* before taking the picture or object out to see what it is.

To teach production of /š/ and /č/:

1. Cut small shoe shapes out of colored paper. Put them in a box and have a child close his eyes and choose a shoe. He can guess its color as the others chant:

New shoes, new shoes,
Which color do you choose?

If the child has found the color he chose, he gets another turn. If not, he loses his turn to the next player.

2. For pronunciation of /č/ make use of the rhythm and stress of verse to help children produce the explosive onset. Teach the finger play "Tom Tinker":

Eye winker (touch eyelid),
Tom Tinker (touch other eyelid),
Nose smeller (touch nose),
Mouth eater (touch lips),
Chin chopper, chin chopper,
Chin chopper, chin (wiggle chin so jaws open and shut very slightly).

Have the children join hands and go around in a circle, chanting:

Charley over the water,
Charley over the sea.
Charley caught a chicken,
But he can't catch me.

When they say *me,* the children squat before the player who is "it" catches them.

Individual activities.

TO TEACH DISCRIMINATION BETWEEN /š/ AND /č/:

1. Say pairs of words and ask individual children if they are "the same" or "different":

chair:chair (the same),
shoe:chew (different)
ship:ship (the same)

2. Have several pictures of words containing either a /š/ or /č/ sound and a chart with two pockets. One picture of an object whose name contains the distinctive sound, such as *sheep* and *chicken,* may be pasted over each of the pockets, or the letters *sh* and *ch* can be used. Children should sort the pictures into the appropriate pockets on the chart.

TO TEACH PRODUCTION OF /š/ AND /č/:

1. Hold a feather in front of your mouth and it will jump for /č/ but blow steadily for /š/. Let all of the children who have difficulty hearing or making the difference between /š/ and /č/ try this "feather test" so they can see a difference.

2. On fish shapes put pictures of objects whose names contain /š/ or /č/ sounds cut from tagboard or construction paper. Put a paper clip on each fish and use a magnet attached to a string for the fishing pole. Children individually catch a fish, saying, *My fish is a* _____.

Older students. The primary goals in this area for older students are the recognition of meaningful differences in the English sound system, and the correlation of these differences with spelling conventions.

Group activities.

TO TEACH DISCRIMINATION OF SOUNDS:

1. Play a tape-recorded passage and have students listen for all of the words which contain one agreed-on sound. They should write down every word they hear which contains the sound. Let several English-speaking students read their lists out loud as a pronunciation model, and for the class to check or add to.

2. Have students set up two columns on a piece of paper; one for each pair of similar sounds (such as, /š/:/č/; /u/:/o/; /i/:/ɪ/, etc.). Read a list of words and have the students check the sound in the pair which they hear. (Teaching a few phonetic symbols to students makes referring to sounds much easier.) For instance:

Teacher:	Students' papers:	i	ɩ
beat		X	
bit			X
whistle			X
feed		X	

TO RELATE SOUNDS TO SPELLING:

1. Use a passage from a book instead of a tape recording as students search for all the words with one agreed-on sound, so that students can see the correct spelling of each word that they list. Lists for different sounds can be compared and spelling regularities induced in class discussion.

2. List pairs of words that differ only in one sound (*washing:watching; base:vase; boot:boat*). Say one sentence for each pair (*Mary is washing the clothes; Pete stole the vase; He saw a boot*) and have students identify the word that they hear.

Individual activities.

TO TEACH SOUND AND SPELLING:

1. Have students compile lists of words in English which contain sounds they have difficulty differentiating. These problem areas can be easily identified in the types of group discrimination activity described above.

2. Let students see, as well as hear, new vocabulary when it is introduced in subject areas. If students are to see a film or hear a lecture, distribute to limited-English-speakers an advance list of words they should know, preferably in the order in which the words will be heard. Review the pronunciation and meaning of important new words with students individually, providing translation if possible when meaning is not clear.

READING

Young children.   If initial reading is to be in English, the reading readiness skills of visual discrimination and auditory discrimination should be provided in the English language activities. Additional goals for young children are learning sound–symbol relationships (*phonics*) and beginning reading of labels and charts.

Group activities.

TO TEACH VISUAL DISCRIMINATION:

1. Have two sets of labels for objects in the classroom. Attach one set to the objects named. Show the second set to the class and have children find the labels (and objects) which match them.

2. Use letter blocks from a Scrabble game. Give each child in the group six or seven letters to place on a rack. Call the name of a letter and have each child remove that letter from his rack if he has it. The first child to remove all his letters may call them out as this activity is repeated. (If children have not yet learned letter names, they can look at the letter called and try to find one on their rack that matches it.)

TO TEACH AUDITORY DISCRIMINATION:

1. Put small items, such as beans, cotton, seeds, or buttons, in pill bottles covered with adhesive paper. Have children take turns shaking two bottles and deciding if they sound "the same" or "different." The children may look inside to check their answers. (Important at this stage is teaching the meaning of *same* and *different*.)

2. Play two sounds in sequence on a tape recorder and have the children decide whether they are made by the same animal, person, or object.

3. Say pairs of words and ask if they are the same or different: *boy:girl*; *baby:baby*; *yellow:white*; *dog:dog*. Remember that sometimes the pair of words should be the same, and continue with many examples.

4. Say pairs of words beginning with the same sound and ask if the beginning sounds are the same or different: *man:milk*; *meat:money*; *monkey:more*. Some children may respond "different" because the members of a pair are different words. Repeat with various examples until the children understand that the words begin with the same sound. Then say more pairs of words, including some which do not start with the same sound and ask if the beginning sounds are the same or different. Continue for a variety of sounds over a period of several days.

5. Paste small pictures on 3 × 5 cards. Using pictures of objects that begin with two or three different sounds, have children sort them into a pocket chart or into piles according to which start the same. Always review the names of the objects which are pictured so that children who do not know the words in English will learn them and still

be able to participate in the sorting activity while vocabulary learning is as yet incomplete.

TO TEACH SOUND/SYMBOL RELATIONSHIPS ("PHONICS") :

1. Follow these steps with a group that includes children who are very limited in English:[1]

> Show pictures of objects that begin with a single letter, such as *m*. The children say the words.
>
> Tell the children that the letter *m* is the first letter of each word. Since the words begin with the same sound, they begin with the same letter. Hold up a flash card with an *m* on it and repeat the words.
>
> Give each child a flash card with *m* and tell him to hold it up every time he hears a word that begins with that letter. Repeat the words again.
>
> Repeat the last three steps with another letter, such as *b*.
>
> Give each child two flash cards, one with *m* and one with *b*. Show pictures of words that begin with one or the other letter and ask the children to hold up the first letter of each word.
>
> Add a third letter in the same manner.

Do not require discrimination of more than three sounds in the early stages. When a fourth letter is added, drop the first, and so forth. Stop often to review all sounds and letters which have been presented. This can be accomplished in activities of the following types:

2. Have children draw and cut out pictures for a class chart for each sound. Print the appropriate letter at the top of the chart and the word beginning with that letter under each picture.

3. With the children's assistance, sort objects according to beginning sounds and put each set in a different bag or box. Let children guess what they will pick from a box or bag without looking. They will only know in advance what letter it starts with, and what sound.

TO TEACH BEGINNING READING OF LABELS AND CHARTS:

1. Label objects in the classroom, or label them with appropriate color words: *brown* on a desk, *black* on a blackboard, and *red* on a ball, for instance.

[1]This sequence was suggested by Dr. John C. Manning of the University of Minnesota when he was a reading consultant to the Clovis Unified School District of Fresno County, California. Many of the activities for young children suggested in this section were developed for use at the kindergarten level of that district and for the Bilingual-Bicultural Kindergarten Project of the Navajo Area of the Bureau of Indian Affairs.

2. Use any of the words introduced in activities for vocabulary development for experience charts or other early reading activities. This will insure that the children just learning English will have already encountered the words aurally (and orally) first.

3. Use a substitution technique with flash cards and a pocket chart, substituting only one word at a time in a basic sentence pattern:

We can *walk*.
We can *run*.
We can *hop*.
He can hop.
She can hop.
(Name) can hop.

A picture on one side of a card and the word on the other are useful when nouns are being learned.

Individual activities.

TO TEACH VISUAL DISCRIMINATION:

Mark letters on a tray jigsaw puzzle, printing letters on the backs of the puzzle pieces and printing the matching letters on the places in the tray where the pieces fit. When beginning to work on a puzzle, the child should turn each piece picture side down so the letter side is up and ready to be fitted into the place in the tray where the matching letter appears. Upper and lower case letters may also be matched to one another in this type of activity. Pairs which will require teaching are *A:a; B:b; D:d; E:e; G:g; M:m;* and *R:r.*

TO TEACH AUDITORY DISCRIMINATION:

Let interested children cut pictures from magazines or catalogues and sort and paste them according to which begin with the same sound. If there are native English-speaking children in the group, they will provide labels for objects that the limited-English-speakers do not know.

TO TEACH SOUND/SYMBOL RELATIONSHIPS:

1. Paste small pictures of objects on 3 × 5 cards and on the other side write the letter that the word designating each object begins with. Pairs of children may use the cards to review the sounds and symbols they have learned. One child shows the pictures and the other tells what the first letter is. Since the letter is written on the back, the

first child can check the other. This is most productive when each pair includes one native English-speaker who can provide the names of objects as needed; this does not detract from the success of the limited-English-speaker who, given that hint, can still name the initial letter.

2. Cut fish shapes from colored construction paper and put a paper clip on each fish. Attach a small magnet to a string and stick which can be used as a fishing pole. On one side of each fish paste a small picture representing an object whose name begins with one of the letters to be reviewed. When a child catches a fish, he must name the object pictured and tell what letter the word starts with.

Older students.   The primary reading goals for older students are increasing skills and fluency, and getting information from books and other written resources.

Group activities.

TO INCREASE SKILLS AND FLUENCY:

1.   If students are literate in their native language, encourage extensive reading in it. Books in at least Spanish, French, and German should be available in any medium sized public library, and school districts implementing bilingual programs should normally be acquiring books in the native language of their students for ready access. Many excellent reading materials are available in languages less commonly taught in the United States, but may be a little more difficult to locate.[2]

2. For intensive skill building, use flash cards, transparencies, or some other device which limits the visual image to only a second or two for each sentence. Ask students to distinguish signs of tense, possession, or negation in English, locate words that tell *how many* or *what kind,* or identify the sentence as a statement, question, or command.

TO LEARN TO USE WRITTEN SOURCES OF INFORMATION:

Duplicate several pages from different kinds of reference materials and formulate drills which will have students locate specific entries, answer questions prepared from this limited corpus of information, and briefly summarize facts given for a selected topic. Duplicating pages will enable all students in the group to look at and discuss the same information, but this should be followed with differential assignments depending on English ability and interests.

2Information on materials in uncommon languages may be obtained from the Center for Applied Linguistics, 1611 N. Kent St., Arlington, Virginia 22209.

Individual activities.

TO INCREASE SKILLS AND FLUENCY:

1. Tape record written material (reading lessons or other subjects) so students can associate fluent English pronunciation and inflection with written symbols. Space may be left on the tapes so students can practice reading aloud after the model.

2. Record tapes to be used in conjunction with individualized worksheets. The easiest levels would have students identify the word or sentence they hear by marking it on the paper.

3. Whenever students still have difficulty at the word recognition level of reading, try to present new vocabulary to them *before* they are asked to read it in context. (Unfamiliar words often cause the limited-English-speaker to come to a screeching halt.) Students can look the words up in a dictionary, use them in original sentences, and, if desired, enter each on a 3 × 5 index card to have handy for reference when they need it in reading and for vocabulary review. When the words are encountered in the text, only the structural and semantic context should be new. Guessing word meanings should not be required in a second language until all words within the understanding of students are easily recognized in print.

4. Record tapes to accompany extensive reading material in English. Students should be able to check out the tapes with books from the class collection or the library.

TO LEARN TO USE WRITTEN SOURCES OF INFORMATION:

1. Questions raised by individuals or by the class may collect in a "question box." Students may periodically elect to find information on one of the questions for the group. The questions may relate to a subject studied in class, a confusing aspect of American culture, or the language, culture, or experiences of a particular ethnic group.

2. Give most research assignments to groups of students rather than individuals, so that limited-English-speakers are paired with native speakers as much as possible.

WRITING

Young children.   The goals of writing for young children are learning letter forms, copying, and beginning creative expression.

Group activities.

TO TEACH LETTER FORMS:

1. Use words the children have already learned in initial reading. This will help reinforce the children's reading vocabulary as well as assure meaningful content for writing.

2. Use copying tasks as the first written exercises for children just learning to form letters and words. The words should always have meaning for the children, and the content should be simple enough so they will not practice errors. Note that it is much easier for children to copy accurately from a paper placed next to theirs on the desk or table than from a chart or chalkboard at a distance.

3. Have children copy their names or a simple heading for identification purposes.

4. Underline one word in a sentence and have children copy the sentence substituting another one for it that would still make sense.

Individual activities.

TO BEGIN CREATIVE EXPRESSION:

1. Have children copy a sentence they have read on an earlier occasion and then draw an appropriate illustration.

2. Duplicate words the children recognize from reading lessons and cut them apart. Make them available in a "word box" together with paste and drawing paper. Children can then build their own sentences without having to be concerned about letter formation, and then illustrate their stories. Since many will want a word that's not there, be available to print more words for the children as requested.

Older students.   The sequence of writing skills for older students is mechanics, controlled variation, analogy and paraphrase, and creative writing.

Group activities.

TO TEACH MECHANICS:

1. Use some dictation exercises.

2. Duplicate words with scrambled letters, sentences with scrambled word order, paragraphs with scrambled sentence order, or stories with

scrambled paragraph order—as different activities—and have students unscramble them.

TO TEACH CONTROLLED VARIATION:

1. Duplicate passages from fairly easy reading material, leaving a blank space in each sentence for at least one word which has a low information load. Students should fill in the blanks with words they think the original writer would have used. A slightly more difficult task would involve completing sentences with appropriate phrases or clauses.

2. Prepare a sentence or short paragraph about a single character. Instruct students to change the story so that it is about two characters instead. They should change only the words that really need to be changed.

3. Use other controlled variation activities which require only a change in time, a change in the sex of the characters, or a change from affirmative to negative.

4. Have every student write a single sentence at the top of a separate piece of paper. Pass the papers around the room, with each student adding a new sentence by changing just one word. (The chain may be stopped when each paper has ten sentences.) The student writing the last sentence should read the first and last to the class.

TO TEACH ANALOGY AND PARAPHRASE:

1. Have students make substantive changes, such as a change in topic, in prepared models, while keeping the organization of the paragraph very similar in structure.

2. Present longer models, such as forms for letters or book reports, and have students make relevant adaptations for specific topics or situations.

3. Duplicate sentences from reading or other subject content material and have students write paraphrases. Include reducing complex sentences to summary phrases as a note-taking skill; complete sentences may be written from these notes after the originals have been forgotten.

Individual activities.

TO TEACH MECHANICS:

1. Make sure all students have learned the English alphabetic sequence. Learning to use it in conjunction with the telephone book and yellow pages, rather than just with the dictionary, is important.

2. Introduce such spelling games as Scrabble and ghost.

TO TEACH ANALOGY:

After reading several model paragraphs, have a student order random sentences into a paragraph of similar structure. These sentences could come from a similar model paragraph which the student has not seen in its original form.

TO TEACH CREATIVE WRITING:

1. Present more advanced students a variety of unlabeled paragraphs from various written selections, including textbooks, personal letters, and stories. Have them note different levels of formality, and help them see such attendant structural differences as the use of contractions, sentence length and complexity, and word choice. Emphasize that one style of writing is not inherently better than another; different styles are more appropriate or more effective in different writing contexts.

2. Avoid correcting the mechanics of creative writing efforts. In fact, correction should probably be limited entirely to controlled writing assignments unless a student asks for assistance. Even then, he should be encouraged to write a first draft with no concern for mechanics; he may then choose to check on spelling, punctuation, and word choice before writing a final copy, but this checking or correction should not be imposed as a requirement.

LISTENING

Young children. The listening goals for young children are increased attention, memory, and perceptual ability.

Group activities.

TO INCREASE ATTENTION:

Utilize community resources for listening activities; for example, ask parents or grandparents to tape record stories for the class. (These need not be in English.)

TO IMPROVE MEMORY:

Have the children close their eyes while someone claps, bounces a ball, or makes some other noise several times in succession. Call on an individual child either to say how many times the action was performed or to repeat it the same number of times, and in the same pattern if the rhythm has been varied.

TO INCREASE PERCEPTUAL ABILITY:

1. Tape record sounds around the school and immediate vicinity. Play them for the class and have children identify each location and activity recorded.

2. Record short segments of speech and have the children try to identify the speaker or to say whether two segments are spoken by the same speaker or different ones.

Individual activities.

TO INCREASE ATTENTION:

Let children borrow a tape recorder overnight and bring back to school the sounds around their home: the pet dog barking, baby brother crying, and, hopefully, grandmother telling a story.

TO IMPROVE MEMORY:

1. Duplicate pictures that go with a story and let children cut them out and paste them in proper sequence.

2. Tell short stories and illustrate them with flannelboard pictures. Let children have access to the flannelboard and pictures during unstructured periods to retell the stories to each other or to themselves. Individual flannelboards can be constructed and duplicate pictures made in class so that children may take them home to keep for retelling to family or friends.

3. Instead of sending notes from class to class and to the office, ask children to carry messages orally.

Older students. The listening goals for older students are increased attention and recall, ability to follow directions, and perceptiveness.

Group activities.

TO INCREASE ATTENTION:

1. Take a tape recorder on any class field trip. Use the sounds recorded as the basis for review identification, discussion, or dramatization.

2. Read a prepared text to the class while they fill in a partial outline of its content.

TO INCREASE RECALL:

Give sequences of arithmetic processes orally, such as, *1 plus 8 minus 6 plus 2*. Have the students write their answers so all have a chance to respond.

TO IMPROVE FOLLOWING DIRECTIONS:

1. Give directions orally which contain several parts, such as instructions for an art project or possibly humorous sequences of actions for the group or specified students to follow.

2. Prerecord such directions or test questions with the format of a "Mission Impossible" program: "This tape will self-destruct in three seconds and *cannot be replayed*. Good luck."

TO INCREASE PERCEPTUAL ABILITY:

1. Tape record from TV shows or at the movies ten or more voices of TV or movie personalities, or tape record from news broadcasts voices of persons of local, national, or world importance. Have students list the identities of the speakers in the order in which the voices are played.

2. Give students an opportunity to hear a number of varieties of English speech. Be sure different regional varieties are represented, as well as both sexes and different social categories.

Individual activities.

TO INCREASE ATTENTION AND RECALL:

1. Record selections from textbooks for individual students to listen to. Have an accompanying worksheet with questions which require them to remember details. Questions may be of the true–false type, or may ask whether the information was included or not included in the selection heard.

2. Record longer selections (perhaps for more fluent speakers in the same class) and provide duplicated sheets with questions to be answered as students listen, or with a partial outline of the content for students to complete while listening.

3. For more advanced students, use similar selections and worksheets sequentially, rather than concurrently, to require recall.

TO INCREASE PERCEPTUAL ABILITY:

Record sentences with a noise (a click or a beep) in place of a key word. These sentences should be of different degrees of complexity for different levels of English proficiency. Some missing words should require hearing the context which follows before identifying and writing them.

SPEAKING

Young children. The primary goal for young children in speaking is to encourage them to talk more, and with less self-consciousness. Several of the activities below are techniques *not* to use, techniques which *inhibit* the development of competence in speaking.

Group activities.

TO ENCOURAGE TALKING:

1. Let the children choose a magazine to look through for a picture they would like to tell a story about. They may sit in pairs and practice telling each other about their pictures and then tell about their pictures to the rest of the class or record their stories on tape. Taped stories and pictures in sequence constitute a creative filmstrip.

2. Have children retell a variety of stories they have heard in class using the same pictures, hand or stick puppets, or flannelboard characters. Encourage the use of such English sequence signals as *first, then,* and *last.*

TO AVOID INHIBITING SPEECH:

1. *Don't* have "Show and Tell," in which a few students each day show things from home and tell the others about them. Particularly in a heterogeneous group, this activity gives the most speaking opportunity to the children who are likely to need it least, and sharpens the social boundaries between those who get new toys and those who have nothing they want to show. Children do enjoy bringing things to school, however, and you can offer all the children in the class this opportunity in other simple activities. For example, each child can contribute a simple object, such as a flower or a piece of candy, to the *"yellow* table" when that color is being taught, or collecting bottle caps for a counting lesson, or bring rocks to class for comparative sizing. Describing and guessing objects the teacher has hidden in a bag is a more efficient way than "Show and Tell" to use time alloted for oral language development, if the entire group is being considered.

2. *Don't* enforce the absolute requirements that students raise their hands before speaking and that only one person talk at a time. These requirements are useful to protect the right of all children to be heard

and to maintain order and reasonable quiet, but exceptions should be allowed whenever the children are really *interested* in a discussion. At such times it is appropriate for speakers to interrupt each other with questions and comments, and the artificial classroom procedures should be suspended in favor of natural language usage.

3. *Don't* have you-can-hear-a-pin-drop quiet in the classroom. Do permit informal verbalization and communication. Natural but quiet talking should accompany schoolwork.

Individual activities.

TO ENCOURAGE TALKING:

1. Have telephones in the classroom. Play telephones are usable, but battery-operated ones provide the additional incentive of two-way conversations between children or between teacher and child.

2. Make a tape recorder available for experimentation and use. (Cassette recorders are much more easily controlled by children than reel-to-reel models.)

FOR THE CHILD WHO SEEMS TOO SHY TO TALK:

1. Make sure he feels as secure as possible in school, and that he succeeds in most tasks he does attempt.

2. If possible, explain things to him in his native language, or ask questions in his language to make sure he understands.

3. Let him sit next to a child who can understand and speak his native language; in no case put him next to a very aggressive student.

4. Do not put him on the spot, for example, in a position of having to talk in front of the class before he is able to talk with individuals in it.

5. Allow him opportunities to respond nonverbally in group activities as soon as he seems ready. He will be willing to respond to *Show me the circle* before he responds to *What is the name of this shape?*

6. Introduce simple puppets to the class and let the shy child talk holding one up in front of his face—to someone else with one in front of him. If the child isn't yet willing to do this, let him hold the puppet while you stand behind and talk for him.

7. Refer him to the school nurse for a hearing test. It will be best if he is not taken out by himself, but with one or two other children.

8. Don't assume that he is "nonverbal." Maintain a positive attitude toward the child and a pleasant environment for him at school, and *be patient.*

Older students.   Goals for older students in speaking include developing skills in storytelling and giving directions, and increased fluency and self-confidence. Again, some activities described below are what *not* to do so that speaking is not inhibited.

Group activities.

TO DEVELOP SKILLS IN STORY TELLING:

1. Tell the students an incomplete short story and ask them to suggest ways it might end.

2. Take photographic slides of field trips and special school functions to use in bilingual language activities. Have the students prepare taped "sound tracts" in two languages and show them to other classes, the PTA, or at open house activities.

TO DEVELOP SKILLS IN GIVING DIRECTIONS:

Build a table-top map of the neighborhood to be used for giving directions to students' homes or to such landmarks as the police station, post office, and public library. One student should give directions verbally (without pointing), and another "walk" with his fingers or "drive" a toy car. The task is more difficult if the student giving directions cannot look at the map. His success is determined by how close the pedestrian or car gets to the desired location.

TO AVOID INHIBITING SPEECH:

1. Relax absolute requirements for hand-raising or quiet in the classroom, as with young children. Remembering that there are individual differences in learning-styles, allow students to seek and give assistance to one another while doing schoolwork (except perhaps in testing situations).

2. *Don't* allow "challenges" by classmates. The practice of encouraging students to challenge the form or content of other students' answers to questions or of their formal oral reports can be particularly damaging to the poise of less confident speakers. Appropriate forms of disagreement should always be available to students, but these must include respecting others' opinions. It is probably best to say that deviations in pronunciation and grammatical usage should *never* be subject to peer challenge and correction. Teachers should not correct the usage of students when they are speaking for communicative or expressive purposes. Deviations from generally accepted forms made on these occasions may be unobtrusively noted and may guide your selection of

usage practices in a more formal context for individual students who need it.

Individual activities.

TO DEVELOP SKILLS IN STORY TELLING:

1. Lend a tape recorder to students and let them collect stories from their parents and grandparents to bring back to class. Stories may be practiced and retold by the students or transferred to written form to constitute highly relevant reading material. (All stories need not be in English.)

2. Let a student who has written or told a good story prepare it for presentation to some younger children. Helping him prepare will include encouraging him to discuss what words might be too hard for the younger children and what parts will interest them most.

OTHER DIMENSIONS OF COMMUNICATION

Young children. Other communicative features of English which young children need to learn include the nature and function of intonation and gestures.

Group activities.

TO TEACH THE MEANING OF INTONATION:

1. Have children listen to a variety of familiar sounds and determine which are *loud* or *soft* and which *high* or *low*. Play recorded speech samples and have them determine the same features.

2. Play a number of tape-recorded segments of speech expressing anger, excitement, and pleasure. Children should learn to tell from each how the speaker feels.

TO TEACH THE MEANING OF GESTURES:

1. Play guessing games in which individuals describe an object with gestures alone and others guess its identity. Commands for different actions may also be given and followed without using speech.

2. Act out such emotional states as *sad, angry,* and *happy* with different facial expressions and gestures. The children should learn to recognize what mood is being portrayed. Photographs or pictures can be

used, but many children may not be able to recognize emotions in these two-dimensional representations.

Individual activities.

TO TEACH THE MEANING OF INTONATION AND GESTURES:

1. Provide hats, play clothes, and other props for role-playing. Encourage the children to imitate adults and other children at home and school, including how they act and sound in specified situations.

2. Make sure each child understands the nonverbal expressions that are used in English to express teasing, affection, humor, or displeasure. Each should also understand that raising the voice level in the classroom is a natural vocal projection teachers use when speaking to a group, and is not an expression of anger.

Older students.   Older students should learn both to recognize and to use nonverbal communication signals of all kinds, verbal structures which do not always take a literal interpretation, and "polite" forms common to classroom contexts.

Group activities.

TO TEACH NONVERBAL COMMUNICATION SIGNALS:

1. Conduct a lesson in mathematics or some other subject area through pantomime—without using speech at all.

2. Provide pictures of people talking. From the visual cues alone, have students guess what each might be saying.

3. Play guessing games in which students act out the meanings of words. Expand to include feelings, with students demonstrating the feelings with gestures and facial expressions. The students may write their guesses (so that all participate at once), and then compare their impressions.

4. Students might like to try expressing an emotion in a language some of the students don't speak and find out to what extent communication is possible on this level without a common language. The activity could lead to valuable discussions of misunderstandings.

TO TEACH VERBAL EXPRESSIONS WHICH DO NOT ALWAYS
TAKE A LITERAL INTERPRETATION:

In game and role-playing formats, let students try out different uses of language in politeness formulas, in mitigation of anger, in lying, or in "putting someone on." Include discussions of how such contexts would be expressed differently in another language and culture.

Individual activities.

TO TEACH THE POLITE OR INDIRECT COMMAND FORMS
WHICH ARE COMMON TO CLASSROOM CONTEXTS:

Use role-playing activities with native English-speaking students taking part to help convey appropriate "school-language" forms and functions. These include apparent statements (*John, it's cold in here,* really meaning *Close the window!*), questions (*Wouldn't you like to get back to work now?* really meaning *Get back to work!*), and compliments (*I like the way Mary is sitting,* really meaning *Sit down, Joe!*). If a student with limited competence in English does not do what he is told to do, be sure he understands that a command has been given.

FOR ADDITIONAL READING

FINOCCHIARO, MARY, *English as a Second Language: From Theory to Practice* (New York: Simon and Schuster, 1964).

————, *Teaching English as a Second Language,* rev. ed. (New York: Harper and Row, 1969).

JOHNSON, FRANCIS C., *English as a Second Language: An Individualized Approach* (Queensland, Australia: Jacaranda Press, 1973).

RIVERS, WILGA M., "Talking Off the Tops of Their Heads," *TESOL Quarterly,* 6 (March 1972), 71–82.

————, *Teaching Foreign-Language Skills* (Chicago: The University of Chicago Press, 1968).

SCHUMANN, JOHN H., "Communication Techniques for the Intermediate and Advanced ESL Student," in *On TESOL 74,* eds. Ruth Crymes and William Norris (1975), pp. 231–36.

SAVILLE-TROIKE, MURIEL, "Reading and the Audio/Lingual Method," *TESOL Quarterly,* 8 (December 1973).

The Role of ESL
in Bilingual Education

CHAPTER 8

The title for this chapter could have taken at least two different forms: "The Role of ESL *and* Bilingual Education," a coordinate structure implying "separate but equal" status, or "The Role of ESL *versus* Bilingual Education," a dichotomous structure implying competition and mutual exclusion. Either of these would have been very misleading, however, and would have indicated a serious misunderstanding of the present function of one field or the other. The choice of the preposition *in* for the title was a very deliberate one, for it expresses the part-to-whole relationship which needs to be recognized and further developed in American education today.

HISTORICAL PERSPECTIVE

Contrary to this present situation, some of the historical aims and means in English language teaching were not at all compatible with the maintenance of other languages and cultures in the United States. The education of Native Americans, for instance, was created to alienate children from their own people. The use of American Indian languages was forbidden, and English was imposed as the sole medium of instruction. In the 1880s, the Commissioner of Indian Affairs stated:

> The first step to be taken toward civilization, toward teaching the Indian the mischief and folly of continuing in their barbarous practices, is to teach him the English language. . . . we must remove the stumbling-blocks of hereditary customs and manners, and of those language is one of the most important.[1]

The still-lingering resentment against United States imperialism in Puerto Rican education is understandable when we read of the language policy imposed on that island in the first half of this century:

> The unifying effects of a language are strong. A double language practice is disintegrating in effect. . . . One of the handicaps to uniformity of language usage is the unwillingness of the older generation to cooperate for the benefit of their children and the nation at large. . . . Since the United States is a major nation of the world, Porto Rico can well get the pace from a growing and ascending nation and learn the expression of the ways of a great people.[2]

The scars left from such ethnocentrism in second language teaching have not yet been erased.

We need not go back so far in our history to find examples of linguistic bias, nor of the damage it did to minority-group students. Many adults today can remember being punished for speaking another language at school—even if they were out on the playground—and as recently as the 1960s teachers were threatened with dismissal for using their students' language to introduce school procedures and concepts, even when the students were five- or six-year-old children badly in need of comfort and reassurance in a strange English-speaking context. As late as 1970, it was still against the law in many states to use any language but English for instruction.

The results of this historically repressive policy have been mixed. Many of the American Indian languages that were spoken in the United States at the end of the nineteenth century have become extinct, or have no speakers left under the age of fifty; many thousands of second generation Americans cannot communicate with their grandparents, and are ashamed of the "broken English" their immigrant parents speak; many thousands more speak their native language only in the limited contexts of home and community, and are unable to read or to write it, or to express themselves in wider contexts of communication. On the

---

[1]Brewton Berry, *The Education of American Indians: A Survey of the Literature* (Columbus: The Ohio State University, 1968) ; ERIC No. ED 026 545.

[2]Henry Cremer, "Spanish and English in Porto Rico," *School and Society*, 36 (S 10, 1932), 338.

other hand, the latest census shows that a larger percentage of Navajo children are learning their ancestral language than did ten or twenty years ago; Puerto Rico is still very much a Spanish-dominant commonwealth; and there are communities of immigrants across the United States who are maintaining their native languages and cultures—in some cases, a hundred years or more after settlement in this country.

Some of the linguistic groups which assimilated under the period of the English-only policy are satisfied to have done so, but there is a strong and pervasive feeling in opposition to the results. This was clearly expressed by an American Indian woman at a recent educational conference who said, "You took our language away. Give it back!" There is a growing desire for cultural revival and maintenance among our citizens which has called for a major shift in language policy as it relates to the education of minority groups.

LEGISLATION

The passage of the Bilingual Education Act (Title VII, Elementary and Secondary Education Act), which was signed into law by President Johnson in 1968, signaled such a shift very dramatically. Millions of dollars have since been spent on programs, and the adoption of state legislation supporting or mandating bilingual education has made it one of the most rapidly growing educational movements in this century. The growth of bilingual education programs has been given further impetus by the landmark Supreme Court decision in the case of Lau vs Nichols (1974), and by various court decrees based on it.[3]

From this legislative perspective we also ask, what is the role of ESL in relation to bilingual education in this country? It is important first of all to set aside the unfortunate misconception that bilingual education and ESL are somehow opposed to one another. Bilingual education, as defined in the legislation, refers to education in two languages, one of which is English. Since ESL, also by definition, concerns teaching English as a second language, it must necessarily be an inherent part of a bilingual program for students whose native language is other than English. The notion of an opposition between the two derives in part from the older concept of ESL as a "pull-out" or segregated program divorced from the curriculum, which concentrated solely on the acquisition of English skills without consideration for the child's native language and culture, and in part from the fact that certain persons preferred such a

---

[3] See the Appendix for the text of the Lau vs. Nichols decision.

program, either because it seemed administratively simpler or because it satisfied assimilationist goals. The new ESL which has been described in this book rejects many past practices as psychologically damaging and educationally unsound, and readily forms a harmonious part of a well-designed bilingual–bicultural education program.

COMPATIBLE ROLES

If we accept this as the appropriate role for ESL in relation to bilingual education, how should the ESL component function? What does it contribute, and how does it correlate with native language instruction?

Goals.   Both ESL and bilingual education are concerned with students' cognitive, social, and psychological development. The ESL component takes primary responsibility for that part of learning that takes place through the medium of the English language, that requires English language skills for acquisition and expression.

Because concepts learned in either language readily transfer to expression in the other, as do such processes as reading, most instructional goals will be general ones for a bilingual program, and not language-specific. Instruction in both languages is aimed at the same ends. The language learning goal should be the shared one of balanced bilingualism—developing listening, speaking, reading, and writing skills in two languages.

Methods.   In this area there are very real differences between the components of a bilingual program, for teaching concepts through a second language medium requires significantly different methods than teaching in the first. The relationship of the students' two language systems must be considered, the learning environment structured to create optimal conditions for learning a second language, and there must be sensitivity to cultural differences in conceptual categorization, experience, and learning-styles which the two languages may reflect.

Concepts do not have to be taught twice; they are introduced in one language, and then only additional labels for them need to be learned in the other. Very close coordination of the nature, scope, and sequence of subject matter presentation in both language components of a bilingual program is thus absolutely essential.

Personnel.   Each teacher in a bilingual program should be qualified to teach in both the students' native language and in English as a second language; conversely, each ESL teacher should be able to teach both in English as the students' second language and in their first language. Ideally, the bilingual teacher and the ESL teacher are one and the same.

An acceptable alternative is a team teaching situation in which one teacher teaches in the first language and one in the second. To be effective each of these two teachers must have some knowledge of the other language. The ESL teacher in this case will have responsibility for content taught through English, and the development of second language skills. The native language teacher will teach content through the first language, develop native language skills, and provide translation support as needed to assure that the second language content is meaningful. This must truly be a *team* effort, with joint planning of complementary content and activities.

A completely *un*acceptable alternative for bilingual education is the monolingual English-speaking teacher and the bilingual aide. The monolingual teacher lacks the essential linguistic competence to develop the students' native language skills, an absolutely basic necessity for bilingual education. Moreover, the socially dominant and prestigious position of the monolingual with respect to the bilingual in such a situation provides a very negative role model for the bilingual students.

Scheduling. *All* teaching done in English when it is a second language is ESL. Care should be taken in a balanced bilingual program which is aiming at development and maintenance of the student's native language that at least equal instructional time be spent in that language.

It is probably best from the standpoint of minimizing interference to schedule some subjects and time slots exclusively in the native language and some exclusively in English (except when translation is needed to clarify meaning). Teaching the same concepts twice ignores their transferability across languages and is a waste of time.

Deciding what content is going to be taught in which language is a critical decision in bilingual scheduling, and one which should be carefully coordinated across grade levels as well as between teachers of the same class. The decision is often based on available materials in each language, especially in intermediate and upper grades. Because mathematics and science content is almost always taught in English at advanced levels in this country, it is probably best also to use these domains as the content for English instruction in the primary grades, so that adequate vocabulary for advanced study of these subjects in English will be developed.

The most important thing to remember in bilingual scheduling is that both languages must be media *through* which subject content is learned—*not* merely systems to be learned in and of themselves.

INDEPENDENT NEED FOR ESL

In addition to the integral function of ESL as part of bilingual education, there remain situations in which, for a variety of reasons (largely practical), ESL programs alone are needed or justified.

First, there are thousands of immigrants who *want* and need to learn English in order to become part of our American society, in order even to earn a living in the United States, and efficient ESL programs can fill these needs.

Also, there are classes composed of students who respectively speak ten to fifteen different languages natively. To provide a specific example, in a recent survey of schools in the District of Columbia, one elementary school reported having sixty-three non-English-speaking students enrolled, including: fourteen speakers of Spanish; eight of French; six Chinese; four Korean; three Hindi; two each Nigerian, Laotian, Italian, Swiss-German, German, and Twi; and one each Ndu, Vietnamese, Hausa, Amharic, Meuda, Swedish, Russian, Portuguese, Czech, Dutch, Japanese, Indonesian, and one other unspecified African language. Such heterogeneous enrollment is not atypical of such ports of entry as Washington, New York, Boston, Seattle, and San Francisco, or even Chicago in the Midwest.

It might be feasible to bus the Spanish, Chinese, and French speakers in this school to centers for bilingual instruction, but such facilities (except for Spanish speakers) do not now exist. The common instructional need which *can* be met at this time is ESL. Even in this case, however, it would be helpful and feasible to provide some bilingual support in *each* student's native language. Particularly when students enter the intermediate and secondary levels with little or no English, they should at least have access to tape recordings explaining the content of lessons in their dominant language, perhaps recorded by bilingual parents, by professors or foreign students in nearby universities, or by others in the community.

Such translation support is only a transition to monolingual instruction in English and not full bilingual education, but it can allow students to follow the gist of class discussion in English sooner, and let them continue their education while they are acquiring some familiarity with our primary language of instruction. If English does not have meaning for these students, learning cannot take place.

Not only is ESL an essential component of bilingual education, but also instruction and explanation in the native language contribute significantly to the effectiveness of ESL.

FOR ADDITIONAL READING

ANDERSSON, THEODORE and MILDRED BOYER, *Bilingual Schooling in the United States* (Austin, Texas: Southwest Educational Development Laboratory, 1970).

ENGLE, PATRICIA LEE, *The Use of Vernacular Languages in Education,* Papers in Applied Linguistics: Bilingual Education Series, No. 3 (Arlington, Va.: Center for Applied Linguistics, 1975).

GAARDER, A. BRUCE, "Organization of the Bilingual School," *Journal of Social Issues,* 23 (1967), 110–20.

GEFFERT, HANNAH N., RORERT J. HARPER II, SALVADOR SARMIENTO, and DANIEL M. SCHEMBER, *The Current Status of U.S. Bilingual Education Legislation,* Papers in Applied Linguistics: Bilingual Education Series, No. 4 (Arlington, Va.: Center for Applied Linguistics, 1975).

LAMBERT, WALLACE E. and G. RICHARD TUCKER, *Bilingual Education of Children: The St. Lambert Experiment* (Rowley, Mass.: Newbury House, 1972).

ORTEGA, LUIS, ed., *Introduction to Bilingual Education* (New York: L. A. Publishing Co., 1975).

PAULSTON, CHRISTINA BRATT, *Implications of Language Learning Theory for Language Planning: Concerns in Bilingual Education,* Papers in Applied Linguistics: Bilingual Education Series, No. 1 (Arlington, Va.: Center for Applied Linguistics, 1974).

SAVILLE, MURIEL R. and RUDOLPH C. TROIKE, *A Handbook of Bilingual Education,* rev. ed. (Washington, D.C.: Teachers of English to Speakers of Other Languages, 1971).

UNITED STATES COMMISSION ON CIVIL RIGHTS, *A Better Chance to Learn: Bilingual-Bicultural Education,* Publication 51 (Washington, D.C.: U.S. Government Printing Office, May 1975).

VON MALTITZ, FRANCES WILLARD, *Living and Learning in Two Languages: Bilingual-Bicultural Education in the United States* (New York: McGraw-Hill, 1975).

Preparation for Teaching

CHAPTER 9

The teaching of English to speakers of other languages in this country has a long tradition, reflected in part in the memorable stories of Mr. H*Y*M*A*N K*A*P*L*A*N.[1] The focus of effort historically was on the adult immigrant in the city, to help him become a productive member of society assimilated into the American mainstream. While this still forms a continuing area of work, which has rarely received the level of recognition it deserves, it has been overshadowed since World War II, first by the emphasis given to teaching English abroad or to foreign students in our colleges, and later to teaching students of limited English-speaking ability (LESA) in our public schools. The awareness of the needs of this last group, and of the needs of teachers who teach them, led in fact to the formation of the TESOL organization in 1966, and to the emergence of ESL as a recognized professional field.

We are now beginning to recognize that many of these developments may have been somewhat untimely, and that the profession must undergo rapid changes if it is to survive and fill a viable educational role today. As we have noted elsewhere, most of the university training programs in ESL have been developed by faculty with experience in teaching English as a *foreign* language, usually to adults. These programs have frequently lacked articulation with regular certification

[1] Leo C. Rosten, *The Education of H*Y*M*A*N K*A*P*L*A*N* (New York: Harcourt, Brace & World, 1937).

requirements in elementary and secondary education, resulting in the production of "specialists" who were trained to teach English in isolation from the remainder of the curriculum and without knowledge of its content. Further, the methods and content taught in these programs were primarily those developed for teaching adults overseas, and little adaptation was made for the age or situational (second versus foreign language) differences of the potential learners.

In addition, the establishment of these programs took place at a time when the behaviorist orientation of the audio/lingual method was still dominant, and teachers have continued to be trained in this methodology long after it has become an anachronism in terms of our understanding of the nature of language and the learning process. Finally, and ironically, the formation of the professional organization of specialists in English as a second language coincided with the beginning of the movement in this country for bilingual education which has largely subsumed ESL in many contexts and has made much of the existing training for ESL teachers even more irrelevant.

Given the recent developments in the field of education, and the growing research evidence that a second language is learned best if it is taught as a medium for content instruction rather than as an end in itself, it is highly questionable whether ESL "specialists" should exist on school staffs.

What, then, should the competencies of the teacher of English as a second language be, and what should be the nature of the teacher preparation program? The following discussion attempts to answer these questions, and to suggest how some of the needed competencies can be acquired.[2]

PREREQUISITES

It should be emphasized at the outset that whatever unique competencies a teacher of English as a second language needs, they must be *in addition to* those that are required for other teachers fo comparable subjects and levels of instruction. In other words, an individual preparing to teach limited-English-speaking students at the elementary level or in a vocational education program should have all of the other basic requirements for an elementary school or vocational education teaching creden-

---

[2]The competencies suggested here for teachers of English as a second language are based on *Guidelines for the Preparation and Certification of Teachers of Bilingual-Bicultural Education,* developed at a conference sponsored by the Center for Applied Linguistics on August 5–6, 1974.

tial. Ideally, states and school districts with sizable limited-English-speaking minorities would require all teachers to have training in second language teaching theory and methods and cross-cultural education.

At a minimum, the teacher of students who are linguistically and culturally different, whether in an all-English program or a bilingual program, must possess the following qualities. He must:

Be genuinely interested in the education of students regardless of their linguistic and cultural background

Be supportive of the goals and processes of multicultural education

Be understanding and accepting of linguistic and cultural diversity

Be respectful of students' personal, family, and community identities

Be sensitive to individual and group needs and feelings

These are not merely platitudes, although they are often recited in an automatic and meaningless fashion. *Teachers without these qualities should not be teaching bilingual students.*

LANGUAGE PROFICIENCY

In working with students for whom English is a second language, the teacher must realize that whatever the subject being taught, whether mathematics, history, or physical education, part of what is being learned is English. The teacher must therefore control a standard variety of English for use in classroom instruction. In defining "standard," however, full allowance must be made for regional variation, as well as for the attitudes of minority groups themselves. Pronunciation is probably the least important consideration (within limits of comprehensibility) since it has the least cognitive significance in instruction.

The teacher must also have or develop an understanding and acceptance of the variety of English used by the students, while of course working toward helping them to acquire a fluent command, in reading, writing, and speaking, of a standard form of English. Difficulty in understanding students' English can best be approached through aural training, using tape recordings of samples of their speech. Criticizing students or embarrassing them by frequent requests for repetition or clarification can inhibit fluency and seriously undermine student–teacher communication.

To the extent possible, the teacher should attempt to develop a basic working ability in the language of the students. A knowledge of students' language can not only serve to increase rapport and improve pedagogical efficiency (by enabling the teacher to provide a more positive learning environment and to supply translations where appropriate), but will also help the teacher to understand better the linguistic and communication problems the students may face. At the same time, by showing an interest in and acceptance of the students' language, the teacher demonstrates that the language is not being disparaged, but instead is being recognized for what it is, a valid means of communication equal in worth to English. This will do more than any words to overcome the erroneous belief that a lack of English proficiency constitutes a cognitive deficit. It has been remarked that only in America can a person be considered educated who knows only one language.

In a multilingual setting, where a half dozen or more languages are represented in a school (or even a single classroom), it is obviously not feasible for a teacher to acquire facility in more than one or two. Even here, however, a few key words can be learned in each, using students themselves as sources of information. In addition, students can be encouraged to teach one another something of their respective languages, and so broaden their linguistic horizons.

The English-speaking teacher in a bilingual program has even greater need to learn the language of the students in order to be able to articulate English-medium course content closely with that in the other language. School districts can assist teachers in acquiring competence in a second language by arranging in-service courses, but by no means should it be assumed that a teacher can be certified as a bilingual teacher after a short course consisting of only a few hundred hours of instruction.

LINGUISTICS

It has long been regarded as essential that a training program for teachers of English as a second language include a significant linguistics component. The basic rationale for this is that a teacher needs an analytic understanding of the nature of language and the structure of English in order to have an adequate grasp of what is being taught and the processes and problems involved in its learning. In large part the insistence on a linguistic component to a training program reflects the leadership of linguists in the development of the field, and a concomitant reaction against the common folk-belief that, unlike other subject areas, no special knowledge is needed to teach English.

It should by now be clear, although it remains to be stated anew for every generation of educators and the general public, that if a teacher is to be able to do more than mechanically teach whatever text-book has been adopted, some detailed knowledge of English and the nature of language and language learning is necessary. Effective curriculum organization, lesson planning, textbook evaluation, and diagnostic–prescriptive teaching are unimaginable without such knowledge.

The requirement of one or more courses in linguistics or even applied linguistics in a training program does not automatically meet this need, however. Because linguistics is a scientific field with its own intrinsic interests and questions, unspecified courses in linguistics may turn out not to have apparent immediate relevance for the language teacher.

It is desirable, therefore, that information from linguistics be presented in terms that are directly germane to the problems of language teaching, and by instructors who are familiar with the immediate needs of teachers in the classroom. Although an understanding of theoretical questions in linguistics or in-depth training in analyzing unwritten languages are valuable goals in themselves, they should be reserved for pursuit by those with a special interest in the subject. Conversely, the teacher should not regard the findings of linguistics as merely a set of facts to memorize for a test and conveniently forget, but should view them as having a relevance which constantly permeates every aspect of teaching. However sterile the presentation of facts, they must come alive in the mind and actions of the teacher.

Minimally, a teacher should have a basic working understanding of:

The nature of language

The nature and significance of language change and variation

The social functions of language and their pedagogical significance

Processes of first and second language acquisition and the nature of bilingualism

The structure of English (phonological, grammatical, and semantic)

Procedures for contrasting English and other languages to predict and diagnose learning problems

CULTURE

Earlier, language was referred to as "the expressive dimension of culture" and the primary medium for transmitting much of culture. The teacher of language is therefore inescapably a teacher of culture. The school is, as we have seen, an instrument of enculturation—and for the student from a different culture, of acculturation. Our very teacher-training is a cultural process. Our culture thus permeates all we do and think and perceive, and it is difficult to escape its all-encompassing influence and hold the mirror up to nature, to see ourselves as others see us. Yet for the teacher of English as a second language, who must be a cross-cultural interpreter, such a step is absolutely necessary.

The concept of and study of culture were first developed in anthropology, and culture remains a central focus of that discipline, although a concern with various aspects of culture may now be found among students of ethnic history and literature, folklore, geography, psychology, and education. A basic understanding of the dimensions of culture can probably best be obtained from a general course in cultural anthropology, but since most anthropologists deal primarily in exotic cultures outside the United States, it will usually remain for the educator to draw the appropriate inferences regarding the relevance to cross-cultural teaching. We have attempted in this book to highlight some of the most important areas of relevance, but this can only be a beginning.

The teacher of English to students from different cultural backgrounds should:

> Understand the nature of culture
>
> Recognize the validity of cultural differences and their importance to identity and self-worth
>
> Be able to identify and distinguish individual and cultural differences in students
>
> Recognize both similarities and differences between Anglo-American and other cultures and their significance for teaching strategies and content
>
> Be able to prepare and assist students to interact successfully in a cross-cultural setting

CURRICULUM AND INSTRUCTION

Since it is both the assumption and the recommendation of this book that the teacher preparing to teach speakers of other languages should integrate the second language instruction with regular curriculum content, whether in a kindergarten class or an adult education program, it follows that the teacher should possess all of the usually expected competencies for the appropriate level, including knowledge of content and methodology, classroom management, lesson planning and organization, utilization of media aids and learning resources, and assessment of student achievement and effectiveness of materials and teaching approaches.

In addition to this, the teacher who has limited-English-speaking students in class, whether as part of a regular program or a bilingual program, should possess the following competencies:

Ability to build second language learning activities on regular curriculum materials

Ability to individualize instructional activities to meet the needs of limited-English-speakers within the heterogeneous class

Ability to adapt teaching strategies and content to take into account differences in culture, styles of learning, and levels of proficiency in English

Ability to identify cultural and linguistic biases and deficiencies in curriculum materials and tests

COMMUNITY RELATIONS

As noted earlier, school achievement and drop-out rates among limited-English-speaking students may be more a factor of socioeconomic status and culture than of language. Different values and lack of familiarity with—and participation in—the institutions of the dominant society, including school, are common among groups of different linguistic and cultural backgrounds.

The teacher can help to bridge the gap between the student's home and school by working with the school administrators and the community leaders to develop parent education programs and bring about more involvement of parents in school activities, both as learning resources and as decision makers. Great cultural sensitivity is often needed in this process if it is to succeed. Training in this important part of a teacher's work should be included in all pre-service and in-service programs.

One of the major failings of traditional education for non-English-speaking and limited-English-speaking students has resulted from the inadequacy of traditional teacher training to prepare teachers to meet the needs of such students. Whether for ESL, bilingual education, or teaching one or a dozen students with limited English competence in a "regular" class, teachers of English as a second language must be better prepared if students are to succeed.

FOR ADDITIONAL READING

ALLEN, HAROLD B., *A Survey of the Teaching of English to Non-English Speakers in the United States* (Urbana, Ill.: National Council of Teachers of English, 1966) .

Blatchford, Charles H., comp., *TESOL Training Program Directory 1974–1976* (Washington, D.C.: Teachers of English to Speakers of Other Languages, 1975).

Finocchiaro, Mary, "The Crucial Variable in TESOL: The Teacher," in *On TESOL 74*, eds. Ruth Crymes and William Norris (Washington, D.C.: Teachers of English to Speakers of Other Languages, 1975).

Guidelines for the Preparation and Certification of Teachers of Bilingual-Bicultural Education (Arlington, Va.: Center for Applied Linguistics, 1974).

Guide to Programs in Linguistics (Arlington, Va.: Center for Applied Linguistics, updated yearly).

Perren, G. E., ed., *Teachers of English as a Second Language: Their Training and Preparation* (New York: Cambridge University Press, 1968); ERIC No. ED 023 087.

Appendix

SUPREME COURT OF THE UNITED STATES

Syllabus

LAU et al. *v.* NICHOLS et al.

CERTIORARI TO THE UNITED STATES COURT OF APPEALS FOR
THE NINTH CIRCUIT

No. 72–6520.   Argued December 10, 1973—Decided January 21, 1974

The failure of the San Francisco school system to provide English language instruction to approximately 1,800 students of Chinese ancestry who do not speak English denies them a meaningful opportunity to participate in the public educational program and thus violates §601 of the Civil Rights Act of 1964, which bans discrimination based "on the ground of race, color, or national origin," in "any program or activity receiving federal financial assistance," and the implementing regulations of the Department of Health, Education, and Welfare. Pp. 2–6.

483 F. 2d 791, reversed.

Douglas, J., delivered the opinion of the Court, in which Brennan, Marshall, Powell, and Rehnquist, JJ., joined. Stewart, J., filed an opinion concurring in the result, in which Burger, C. J., and Blackmun,

J., joined. WHITE, J., concurred in the result. BLACKMUN, J., filed an opinion concurring in the result, in which BURGER, C. J., joined.

SUPREME COURT OF THE UNITED STATES

No. 72–6520

Kinney Kinmon Lau, a Minor by and Through Mrs. Kam Wai Lau, His Guardian ad litem, et al., Petitioners, *v.* Alan H. Nichols et al.	On Writ of Certiorari to the United States Court of Appeals for the Ninth Circuit.

[January 21, 1974]

MR. JUSTICE DOUGLAS delivered the opinion of the Court.

The San Francisco California school system was integrated in 1971 as a result of a federal court decree, 339 F. Supp. 1315. See *Lee v. Johnson,* 404 U. S. 1215. The District Court found that there are 2,856 students of Chinese ancestry in the school system who do not speak English. Of those who have that language deficiency, about 1,000 are given supplemental courses in the English language.[1] About 1,800 however do not receive that instruction.

This class suit brought by non-English speaking Chinese students against officials responsible for the operation of the San Francisco Unified School District seeks relief against the unequal educational opportunities which are alleged to violate the Fourteenth Amendment. No specific remedy is urged upon us. Teaching English to the students of Chinese ancestry who do not speak the language is one choice. Giving instructions to this group in Chinese is another. There may be others. Petitioner asks only that the Board of Education be directed to apply its expertise to the problem and rectify the situation.

The District Court denied relief. The Court of Appeals affirmed, holding that there was no violation of the Equal Protection Clause of

---

[1] A reported adopted by the Human Rights Commission of San Francisco and submitted to the court by respondent after oral argument shows that, as of April 1973, there were 3,457 Chinese students in the school system who spoke little or no English. The document further showed 2,136 students enrolled in Chinese special instruction classes, but at least 429 of the enrollees were not Chinese but were included for ethnic balance. Thus, as of April 1973, no more than 1,707 of the 3,457 Chinese students needing special English instruction were receiving it.

the Fourteenth Amendment nor of § 601 of the Civil Rights Act of 1964, which excludes from participation in federal financial assistance, recipients of aid which discriminate against racial groups, 483 F. 2d 791. One judge dissented. A hearing *en banc* was denied, two judges dissenting. *Id.*, at 805.

We granted the petition for certiorari because of the public importance of the question presented, 412 U. S. 938.

The Court of Appeals reasoned that "every student brings to the starting line of his educational career different advantages and disadvantages caused in part by social, economic and cultural background, created and continued completely apart from any contribution by the school system," 483 F. 2d, at 497. Yet in our view the case may not be so easily decided. This is a public school system of California and § 571 of the California Education Code states that "English shall be the basic language of instruction in all schools." That section permits a school district to determine "when and under what circumstances instruction may be given bilingually." That section also states as "the policy of the state" to insure "the mastery of English by all pupils in the schools." And bilingual instruction is authorized "to the extent that it does not interfere with the systematic, sequential, and regular instruction of all pupils in the English language."

Moreover § 8573 of the Education Code provides that no pupil shall receive a diploma of graduation from grade 12 who has not met the standards of proficiency in "English," as well as other prescribed subjects. Moreover by § 12101 of the Education Code children between the ages of six and 16 years are (with exceptions not material here) "subject to compulsory full-time education."

Under these state-imposed standards there is no equality of treatment merely by providing students with the same facilities, text books, teachers, and curriculum; for students who do not understand English are effectively foreclosed from any meaningful education.

Basic English skills are at the very core of what these public schools teach. Imposition of a requirement that, before a child can effectively participate in the educational program, he must already have acquired those basic skills is to make a mockery of public education. We know that those who do not understand English are certain to find their classroom experiences wholly incomprehensible and in no way meaningful.

We do not reach the Equal Protection Clause argument which has been advanced but rely solely on § 601 of the Civil Rights Act of 1964, 42 U. S. C. § 2000 (d) to reverse the Court of Appeals.

That section bans discrimination based "on the ground of race, color, or national origin," in "any program or activity receiving federal financial assistance." The school district involved in this litigation receives large amounts of federal financial assistance. HEW, which has authority to promulgate regulations prohibiting discrimination in federally assisted school systems, 42 U. S. C. § 2000 (d), in 1968 issued one guideline that "school systems are responsible for assuring that students of a particular race, color, or national origin are not denied the opportunity to obtain the education generally obtained by other students in the system." 33 CFR § 4955. In 1970 HEW made the guidelines more specific, requiring school districts that were federally funded "to rectify the language deficiency in order to open" the instruction to students who had "linguistic deficiencies," 35 Fed. Reg. 11595.

By § 602 of the Act HEW is authorized to issue rules, regulations, and orders[2] to make sure that recipients of federal aid under its jurisdiction conduct any federal financed projects consistently with § 601. HEW's regulations specify, 45 CFR § 80.3 (b)(1), that the recipients may not:

> "Provide any service, financial aid, or other benefit to an individual which is different, or is provided in a different manner, from that provided to others under the program;
>
> "Restrict an individual in any way in the enjoyment of any advantage or privilege enjoyed by others receiving any service, financial aid, or other benefit under the program";

Discrimination among students on account of race or national origin that is prohibited includes "discrimination in the availability or use of any academic . . . or other facilities of the grantee or other recipient." *Id.,* 80.5 (b).

Discrimination is barred which has that *effect* even though no purposeful design is present: a recipient "may not . . . utilize criteria or methods of administration which would have the effect of subjecting individuals to discrimination" or has "the effect of defeating or substantially impairing accomplishment of the objectives of the program

---

[2]Section 602 provides:
"Each Federal department and agency which is empowered to extend Federal financial assistance to any program or activity, by way of grant, loan, or contract other than a contract of insurance or guaranty, is authorized and directed to effectuate the provisions of section 2000d of this title with respect to such program or activity by issuing rules, regulation, or orders of general applicability which shall be consistent with achievement of the objectives of the statute authorizing the financial assistance in connection with which the action is taken. . . ."

as respect individuals of a particular race, color, or national origin."
Id., 80.3 (b(2).

It seems obvious that the Chinese-speaking minority receives less
benefits than the English-speaking majority from respondents' school
system which denies them a meaningful opportunity to participate in
the educational program—all earmarks of the discrimination banned by
the Regulations.[3] In 1970 HEW issued clarifying guidelines (35 Fed. Reg.
11595) which include the following:

"Where inability to speak and understand the English language
excludes national origin-minority group children from effective participation in the educational program offered by a school district, the district
must take affirmative steps to rectify the language deficiency in order to
open its instructional program to these students." (Pet. Br. App. 1a).

"Any ability grouping or tracking system employed by the school
system to deal with the special language skill needs of national origin-
minority group children must be designed to meet such language skill
needs as soon as possible and must not operate as an educational dead-
end or permanent track." (Pet. Br. p. 2a).

Respondent school district contractually agreed to "comply with
title VI of the Civil Rights Act of 1964 . . . and all requirements imposed
by or pursuant to the Regulations" of HEW (45 CFR Pt. 80) which are
"issued pursuant to that title . . ." and also immediately to "take any
measures necessary to effectuate this agreement." The Federal Government has power to fix the terms on which its money allotments to the
States shall be disbursed. *Oklahoma* v. *Civil Service Commission,* 330
U. S. 127, 142–143. Whatever may be the limits of that power, *Steward
Machine Co.* v. *Davis,* 301 U. S. 548, 590 *et seq.,* they have not been
reached here. Senator Humphrey, during the floor debates on the Civil
Rights Act of 1964, said:[4]

"Simple justice requires that public funds, to which all taxpayers
of all races contribute, not be spent in any fashion which encourages,
entrenches, subsidizes, or results in racial discrimination."

We accordingly reverse the judgment of the Court of Appeals and
remand the case for the fashioning of appropriate relief.

Reversed.

MR. JUSTICE WHITE concurs in the result.

[3]And see Report of the Human Rights Commission of San Francisco, Bilingual
Education in the San Francisco Public Schools, Aug. 9, 1973.

[4]110 Cong. Rec. 6543 (Senator Humphrey quoting from President Kennedy's
message to Congress, June 19, 1963.)

SUPREME COURT OF THE UNITED STATES

No. 72–6520

Kinney Kinmon Lau, a Minor
by and Through Mrs. Kam
Wai Lau, His Guardian
ad litem, et al.,
Petitioners,
v.
Alan H. Nichols et al.

On Writ of Certiorari
to the United States
Court of Appeals for
the Ninth Circuit.

[January 21, 1974]

MR. JUSTICE STEWART, with whom THE CHIEF JUSTICE and MR. JUSTICE BLACKMUN join, concurring in the result.

It is uncontested that more than 2,800 school children of Chinese ancestry attend school in the San Francisco Unified School District system even though they do not speak, understand, read, or write the English language, and that as to some 1,800 of these pupils the respondent school authorities have taken no significant steps to deal with this language deficiency. The petitioners do not contend, however, that the respondents have affirmatively or intentionally contributed to this inadequacy, but only that they have failed to act in the face of changing social and linguistic patterns. Because of this laissez faire attitude on the part of the school administrators, it is not entirely clear that § 601 of the Civil Rights Act of 1964, 42 U. S. C. § 2000d, standing alone, would render illegal the expenditure of federal funds on these schools. For that section provides that "[n]o person in the United States shall, on the ground of race, color, or national origin be excluded from participation in, be denied the benefits of, or be subjected to discrimination under a general authorization provision such as § 602 of Tit. VI[1] "will be sustained so

---

[1] Section 602, 42 U. S. C. § 2000d–1, provides in pertinent part:
'Each Federal department and agency which is empowered to extend Federal assistance to any program or activity, by way of grant, loan, or contract other than a contract of insurance or guaranty, is authorized and directed to effectuate the provisions of section 2000d of this title with respect to such program or activity by issuing, rules, regulations, or orders of general applicability which shall be consistent with achievement of the objectives of the statute authorizing the financial assistance in connection with which the action is taken . . . ."
The United States as *amicus curiae* asserts in its brief, and the respondents appear to concede, that the guidelines were issued pursuant to § 602.

long as it is 'reasonably related to the purposes of the enabling legislation.' *Thorpe* v. *Housing Authority of the City of Durham*, 393 U. S. 268, 280–281 (1969)." I think the guidelines here fairly meet that test. Moreover, in assessing the purposes of remedial legislation we have found that departmental regulations and "consistent administrative construction" are "entitled to great weight." *Trafficante* v. *Metropolitan Life Insurance Co.*, 409 U. S. 205, 210; *Griggs* v. *Duke Power Co.*, 401 U. S. 424, 433–434; *Udall* v. *Tallman*, 380 U.S. 1. The Department has reasonably and consistently interpreted § 601 to require affirmative remedial efforts to give special attention to linguistically deprived children.

For these reasons I concur in the judgment of the Court.

SUPREME COURT OF THE UNITED STATES

No. 72–6520

Kinney Kinmon Lau, a Minor by and Through Mrs. Kam Wai Lau, His Guardian ad litem, et al., Petitioners, *v.* Alan H. Nichols et al.	On Writ of Certiorari to the United States Court of Appeals for the Ninth Circuit.

[January 21, 1974]

MR. JUSTICE BLACKMUN, with whom THE CHIEF JUSTICE joins, concurring in the result.

I join MR. JUSTICE STEWART's opinion and thus I, too, concur in the result. Against the possibility that the Court's judgment may be interpreted too broadly, I stress the fact that the children with whom we are concerned here number about 1800. This is a very substantial group that is being deprived of any meaningful schooling because they cannot understand the language of the classroom. We may only guess as to why they have had no exposure to English in their preschool years. Earlier generations of American ethnic groups have overcome the language barrier by earnest parental endeavor or by the hard fact of being pushed out of the family or community nest and into the realities of broader experience.

I merely wish to make plain that when, in another case, we are concerned with a very few youngsters, or with just a single child who speaks only German or Polish or Spanish or any language other than

English, I would not regard today's decision, or the separate concurrence, as conclusive upon the issue whether the statute and the guideline require the funded school district to provide special instruction. For me, numbers are at the heart of this case and my concurrence is to be understood accordingly.